Learn Model Context Protocol with Python

Build agentic systems in Python with the new standard for AI capabilities

Christoffer Noring

‹packt›

Learn Model Context Protocol with Python

Portfolio Director: Ashwin Nair
Relationship Lead: Aaron Lazar
Project Manager: Ruvika Rao
Content Engineer: Runcil Rebello
Technical Editor: Rohit Singh
Copy Editor: Safis Editing
Indexer: Manju Arasan
Proofreader: Runcil Rebello
Production Designer: Shantanu Zagade
Growth Lead: Anamika Singh

First published: October 2025

Production reference: 1171025

Published by Packt Publishing Ltd.
Grosvenor House
11 St Paul's Square
Birmingham
B3 1RB, UK.

ISBN 978-1-80610-323-2

www.packtpub.com

To my wife, without you, I wouldn't be at this point in my life. I owe you everything. Also, to my parents, my biggest fans, your support means the world.

Also, huge thanks to my colleagues at Microsoft for all the help and support, and especially to John Papa and Dan Wahlin for being amazing mentors and friends over the years.

– Christoffer Noring

Foreword

When Christoffer Noring first told me about his idea for a book on the **Model Context Protocol (MCP)**, I was immediately intrigued. The concept of bringing clarity to such a rapidly evolving area of AI felt both timely and necessary. Christoffer has always had a gift for explaining complex technical systems in a way that makes them accessible without oversimplifying. In this book, he channels that clarity into a complete guide to understanding and building AI systems with MCP.

What stands out most to me is the way Christoffer approaches the subject. He doesn't just document how MCP works; he places it in the context of real challenges and walks you through different options to consider. The material is practical, thoughtfully organized, and written with the same curiosity and care that Christoffer brings to his talks and tutorials.

The range of topics, which includes sampling, elicitation, security, server design, and more, shows how MCP supports building AI systems that are both adaptive and reliable. The examples are grounded in real-world use, depicting how design directly impacts the performance and behavior of AI as it interacts with MCP servers and tools.

This book is a practical map for anyone developing AI systems that rely on strong architectural foundations. I'm confident readers will come away not only understanding MCP but also with a deeper appreciation for how thoughtful MCP protocol and tool planning and design can significantly enhance your custom AI systems and impact the way you interact with AI assistants.

Dan Wahlin

Principal Content Engineer, Microsoft

Contributors

About the author

Christoffer Noring is a passionate developer and educator who specializes in modern web technologies and AI integrations and works as an engineer at Microsoft. He's also a tutor at the University of Oxford and is a published author on Angular, RxJs, generative AI, and now MCP. Christoffer has almost two decades of experience in software development and is a frequent speaker at tech conferences worldwide. According to his manager, his best quality is being able to break down complex technical concepts into simple, understandable terms. He hopes you agree! ;)

When not coding or writing, Christoffer is probably growing another user community, mentoring developers, or spending time with his family.

About the reviewers

Mark McDonagh is a seasoned technology executive and information security specialist with over 25 years of experience in enterprise software development, cloud transformation, and cybersecurity governance. He has led high-performing cloud engineering teams in the telecom, contact-center, and airline industries, delivering secure, scalable platforms and overseeing compliance programs. Mark holds a Bachelor's degree in Computer Systems, a Master's in Cybersecurity and Computer Forensics, and a Postgraduate Diploma in Executive Management, and is currently pursuing a Postgraduate in AI/ML.

Outside of work, Mark actively contributes to standards development and cybersecurity education through volunteer roles with standards organizations, most recently with the Cloud Security Alliance's **Customer Communications Management** (**CCM**) and AI initiatives. Mark currently leads Governance and Information Security at Verodat, where he helps shape resilient, AI-driven data platforms and contributes to emerging protocols like the MCP. In his spare time Mark also volunteers to help people in need through his work for the Legion of Mary.

Tejul Pandit is a Senior Staff Machine Learning Engineer with over seven years of experience in the field. She holds a Master's degree in Artificial Intelligence from Northwestern University and is the author of multiple research papers and patents. Her expertise lies in designing and implementing ML-based architectures, including leading the company's first large-scale deployment of an ML model that significantly reduced human effort while maintaining high efficacy. Tejul is actively involved in LLM-based **Retrieval-Augmented Generation** (**RAG**) research, focusing on building efficient RAG systems and effective prompting strategies, and has been invited to present at AI and ML conferences on topics such as building efficient RAG pipelines and enterprise AI applications.

Maxim Salnikov is a leader at the intersection of cloud, web, and artificial intelligence. With over two decades of software engineering experience, he has dedicated his career to empowering developers and shaping the future of technology.

As a Senior Solution Engineer at Microsoft, Maxim is on the front lines of the AI revolution, focusing on next-generation AI-native developer tools and platforms. His influence extends globally through his work as an international speaker and a key organizer for Norway's largest developer communities. A true pioneer in the Generative AI space, he founded the world's first Prompt Engineering Conference, establishing a global platform for innovation in this critical new field.

Table of Contents

Chapter 5: Streamable HTTP   85

Chapter 6: Advanced Servers   109

Chapter 7: Building Clients   131

Chapter 11: Securing Your Application 207

Preface

The **Model Context Protocol (MCP)** represents a revolutionary approach to building **artificial intelligence (AI)** applications that can efficiently distribute resources, standardize capabilities, and facilitate seamless communication between different components in complex systems. As AI continues to evolve and integrate into every aspect of our digital lives, the need for standardized, scalable, and secure protocols becomes increasingly critical.

MCP addresses fundamental challenges that developers face when building AI applications: resource distribution bottlenecks, lack of standardization across different components, complexity in building and testing distributed systems, and the intricate process of developing clients that can effectively interact with servers and **large language models (LLMs)**. By providing a structured framework, MCP enables developers to create more efficient, maintainable, and scalable AI applications.

Among all the protocols and frameworks available for AI application development, MCP stands out because it offers several key advantages:

- It provides a standardized way to describe and communicate capabilities between different system components
- It enables efficient resource distribution across multiple servers, improving performance and scalability
- It offers comprehensive guidelines for building, testing, and deploying both servers and clients
- It supports multiple communication methods, including **standard input/output (STDIO)** and **server-sent events (SSE)**
- It facilitates integration with modern development tools and platforms

In this comprehensive book, we will first explore the foundational concepts of the MCP, understanding its architecture, components, and the problems it solves in modern AI application development.

Once you understand the core protocol concepts, we will dive deep into practical implementation, covering how to build and test MCP servers using various approaches, including STDIO and SSE-based servers. We will also explore advanced server development techniques and patterns that will help you create robust, production-ready applications.

The book then progresses to client development, showing you how to build effective clients both with and without LLM integration, and how to consume MCP servers using popular tools such as Claude Desktop and **Virtual Studio Code (VS Code)** agent mode. We will also cover advanced topics such as sampling and elicitation techniques that can enhance your AI applications.

Finally, we will address critical production concerns, including security best practices, deployment strategies, and scaling considerations that are essential for running MCP applications in real-world environments.

This book will guide you through numerous practical examples and exercises, demonstrating best practices for building MCP applications and providing hands-on experience with real-world scenarios. The examples and code samples are designed to be immediately applicable to your own projects, whether you're building simple proofs of concept or complex enterprise applications.

Throughout the book, we include comprehensive solutions and code examples in Python. The appendix also provides a comprehensive Python primer for those who need to brush up on their Python skills.

> The author acknowledges the use of cutting-edge AI, in this case **GitHub Copilot**, with the sole aim of enhancing the language and clarity within the book, thereby ensuring a smooth reading experience for readers. It's important to note that the content itself has been crafted by the author and edited by a professional publishing team.

Who this book is for

This book is for developers, AI engineers, and software architects looking to build sophisticated AI applications using the MCP. Whether you're a backend developer wanting to create efficient AI servers, a frontend developer looking to integrate AI capabilities into your applications, or an AI researcher exploring new ways to structure AI systems, this book provides the knowledge and practical skills you need.

Basic programming experience in Python is recommended, along with familiarity with web development concepts, API design, and fundamental AI/ML concepts. Experience with modern development tools and practices will help you get the most out of this book.

What this book covers

Chapter 1, Introduction to the Model Context Protocol, introduces the Model Context Protocol, its historical background, and the fundamental problems it solves in AI application development. You'll understand why MCP is essential for modern AI systems.

Chapter 2, Explaining the Model Context Protocol, provides a comprehensive deep dive into the MCP protocol itself, covering its architecture, key components (hosts, clients, servers), communication methods (STDIO and SSE), and the standard capabilities framework.

Chapter 3, Building and Testing Servers, focuses on practical server development using STDIO communication, covering server architecture, resource and tool implementation, and comprehensive testing strategies using inspector tools.

Chapter 4, Building SSE Servers, explores SSE-based server development, showing you how to build real-time, streaming MCP servers for more dynamic applications.

Chapter 5, Streamable HTTP, covers advanced HTTP streaming techniques for MCP servers, enabling you to build highly scalable and efficient server implementations.

Chapter 6, Advanced Servers, delves into sophisticated server patterns, advanced resource management, complex tool implementations, and production-ready server architectures.

Chapter 7, Building Clients, teaches you how to develop MCP clients, both standalone applications and those integrated with LLMs, covering client architecture and best practices.

Chapter 8, Consuming Servers, demonstrates how to effectively use MCP servers through various clients and tools, including Claude Desktop, VS Code agent mode, and custom client implementations.

Chapter 9, Sampling, explores advanced sampling techniques for AI applications, showing how to leverage MCP's capabilities for sophisticated AI interactions and content generation.

Chapter 10, Elicitation, covers techniques for effective information elicitation in AI applications, demonstrating how to design systems that can intelligently gather and process information.

Chapter 11, Securing Your Application, addresses comprehensive security considerations for MCP applications, including authentication, authorization, data protection, and secure communication patterns.

Chapter 12, Bringing MCP Apps to Production, provides practical guidance on deploying MCP applications to production environments, covering scaling strategies, monitoring, and maintenance best practices.

Appendix, Building for the Web with Modern Python, offers a comprehensive primer on advanced Python features specifically relevant to MCP development, including async programming, context managers, type hints, and modern Python patterns.

To get the most out of this book

To follow along with the examples and exercises in this book, you'll need the following:

- Python 3.8 or later installed on your system
- A code editor or IDE (VS Code is recommended)
- Basic familiarity with command-line interfaces
- An understanding of HTTP, JSON, and basic networking concepts
- Access to modern AI tools such as Claude or ChatGPT for testing examples

All the code examples are designed to run on Windows, macOS, and Linux. The book includes specific installation instructions and setup guidance for each major platform.

Download the example code files

You can download the example code files for this book from GitHub at `https://github.com/PacktPublishing/Learn-Model-Context-Protocol-with-Python`. If there's an update to the code, it will be updated in the GitHub repository. We also provide comprehensive examples, solutions to exercises, and additional resources to help you master MCP development.

We also have other code bundles from our rich catalog of books and videos available at `https://github.com/PacktPublishing/`. Check them out!

Download the color images

We also provide a PDF file that has color images of the screenshots/diagrams used in this book. You can download it here: `https://packt.link/gbp/9781806103232`.

Conventions used

There are a number of text conventions used throughout this book.

`Code In Text`: Indicates code words in text, database table names, folder names, filenames, file extensions, pathnames, dummy URLs, user input, and protocol names. For example: "The syntax is `uvicorn <filename>:<name of app instance>`. In this case, the filename is `main.py` and the app instance is app."

A block of code is set as follows:

```python
from starlette.applications import Starlette
from starlette.responses import JSONResponse
from starlette.routing import Route


async def homepage(request):
    return JSONResponse({'hello': 'world'})


app = Starlette(debug=True, routes=[
    Route('/', homepage),
])
```

Any command-line input or output is written as follows:

```
npx @modelcontextprotocol/inspector --cli
http:localhost:8000/sse --method tools/list
```

Bold: Indicates a new term, an important word, or words that you see on the screen. For instance, words in menus or dialog boxes appear in the text like this. For example: "Note how **Transport Type** is set to SSE and **URL** is set to http://localhost:8000/sse."

Warnings or important notes appear like this.

Tips and tricks appear like this.

Get in touch

Feedback from our readers is always welcome.

General feedback: If you have questions about any aspect of this book or have any general feedback, please email us at customercare@packt.com and mention the book's title in the subject of your message.

Errata: Although we have taken every care to ensure the accuracy of our content, mistakes do happen. If you have found a mistake in this book, we would be grateful if you reported this to us. Please visit http://www.packt.com/submit-errata, click **Submit Errata**, and fill in the form.

Piracy: If you come across any illegal copies of our works in any form on the internet, we would be grateful if you would provide us with the location address or website name. Please contact us at copyright@packt.com with a link to the material.

If you are interested in becoming an author: If there is a topic that you have expertise in and you are interested in either writing or contributing to a book, please visit http://authors.packt.com/.

Share your thoughts

Once you've read *Learn Model Context Protocol with Python*, we'd love to hear your thoughts! Scan the QR code below to go straight to the Amazon review page for this book and share your feedback.

https://packt.link/r/1806103230

Your review is important to us and the tech community and will help us make sure we're delivering excellent quality content.

1

Introduction to the Model Context Protocol

Generative AI has rapidly become a force in today's technological landscape, reshaping industries and redefining how we approach problem-solving. From natural language processing to image generation, the integration of generative AI into various domains has opened up new possibilities for innovation and efficiency.

For us developers, integrating generative AI into app development workflows is not without its complexities. We must carefully evaluate factors such as model accuracy, ethical considerations, and computational efficiency.

It's in the process of building applications that we need to consider how we standardize the way we build our AI applications. Standardization means that everything looks the same, which should mean easier integration and collaboration across different teams and tools.

This is where the **Model Context Protocol (MCP)** comes in, to standardize how we ensure that AI-powered applications can easily find what they need from tools, content, and prompts; more on that shortly.

The chapter covers the following topics:

- How we got here, from SOAP to REST to GraphQL to gRPC to MCP
- The need for a standard
- Endless possibilities: know how to prompt, and a world of MCP servers is your oyster
- What is the MCP?

Getting the most out of this book — get to know your free benefits

Unlock exclusive **free** benefits that come with your purchase, thoughtfully crafted to supercharge your learning journey and help you learn without limits.

Here's a quick overview of what you get with this book:

Next-gen reader

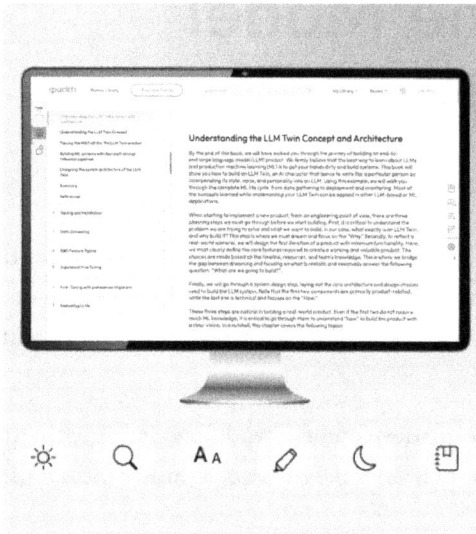

Our web-based reader, designed to help you learn effectively, comes with the following features:

⊘ **Multi-device progress sync**: Learn from any device with seamless progress sync.

📑 **Highlighting and notetaking**: Turn your reading into lasting knowledge.

🔖 **Bookmarking**: Revisit your most important learnings anytime.

✳ **Dark mode**: Focus with minimal eye strain by switching to dark or sepia mode.

Figure 1.1: Illustration of the next-gen Packt Reader's features

Interactive AI assistant (beta)

Our interactive AI assistant has been trained on the content of this book, to maximize your learning experience. It comes with the following features:

✢ **Summarize it**: Summarize key sections or an entire chapter.

✢ **AI code explainers**: In the next-gen Packt Reader, click the **Explain** button above each code block for AI-powered code explanations.

Note: The AI assistant is part of next-gen Packt Reader and is still in beta.

Figure 1.2: Illustration of Packt's AI assistant

DRM-free PDF or ePub version

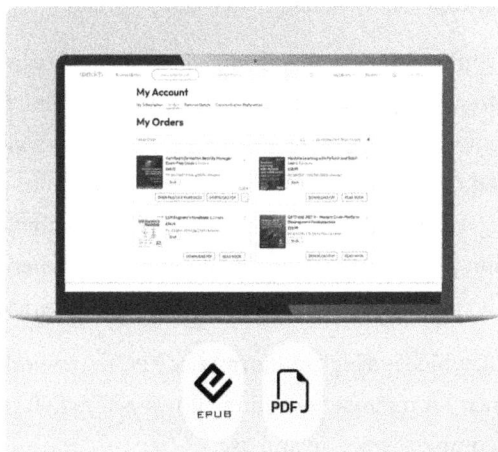

Learn without limits with the following perks included with your purchase:

📑 Learn from anywhere with a DRM-free PDF copy of this book.

📖 Use your favorite e-reader to learn using a DRM-free ePub version of this book.

Figure 1.3: Free PDF and ePub

How we got here, from SOAP to REST to GraphQL to gRPC to MCP

Before we dive into the details of the MCP, let's take a step back and look at how we got here.

One of my early memories of using web requests involved using XML to send and receive data. This was back in the days of **Simple Object Access Protocol (SOAP)**, which was a protocol for exchanging structured information in the implementation of web services. It was great, but it was also very complex and felt heavy.

Then came **Representational State Transfer (REST)**, which was a simpler way to build web services. It used HTTP and JSON, which made it easier to work with. REST was, and is, great.

There's nothing inherently wrong with REST, but you could argue that if you had a backend team and a frontend team, the frontend team would often be waiting for the backend team to finish their work before they could start building the frontend. This is where **GraphQL** came in, which allowed you to query only the data you needed and made it easier to work with APIs. Of course, that creates other problems, such as over-fetching and under-fetching data and what's known as the **N+1 problem**. The N+1 problem is a common performance issue in GraphQL APIs where multiple requests are made to fetch related data, leading to inefficiencies and increased latency.

There's also **Google Remote Procedure Call (gRPC)**, which is a high-performance RPC framework that uses HTTP/2 and Protocol Buffers. gRPC is great for microservices and allows you to define your APIs in a more structured way, but it can be complex to set up and use.

The need for a standard

All of these formats are great in their own right, but they all have their own problems. Also, the problem isn't often of this nature, but rather a string of questions that we need to ask ourselves when building applications:

- **What does this app/API do?** How do we easily expose the capabilities of our applications in a way that is easy to understand and use? Of course, no one has really agreed on a standard for this yet, until now.

- **How do we build apps if prompts are the new way to interact?** Add to that that users are becoming accustomed to using prompts to interact with applications, and you start wondering what part is the generative AI part, and what part is the capabilities of the application itself?

- **Should large language model (LLM) and other capabilities be kept separate?** Also, do I really need the generative AI part and the capabilities of the application to all be in the same place?

- **If they were kept separate, what could we gain?** If we could separate the two, in a client and server part, then maybe we could easily consume servers built by others – *Hello agentic era*.

These are some good questions to ask yourself. But this doesn't answer why we need a standard. Let's look at that further:

- **We, as developers, are too good at programming**: Here's the problem: as developers, we're almost too good at programming, meaning that we're used to gluing different things together. We can build applications that use multiple AI models, and we can make applications talk to each other that use different protocols and formats. This is not always easy, but we can do it.

- **We can do it, but at what cost?** As mentioned, just because we can *glue* virtually anything together doesn't mean we should. Yes, we can wrap anything into a REST API and make it talk to anything else. But how much time and effort does that take?

- **The solution, a standard**: Now, you see the need for a standard, hopefully. The great news is that there is a standard that is being developed to solve this problem. It's called the MCP. This enables you to not only describe your resources and capabilities in a standardized way, but also describe how to interact with them.

That means that you can literally throw the MCP on top of any app and suddenly any client that talks MCP can interact with it. Imagine the following scenario: you have a client, and that client can talk to a number of MCP servers that run both locally and remotely. All of this is made possible because you listed these servers in an `mcp.json` file.

Suddenly, you have access to tools to access anything you can imagine, from databases to cloud providers to any other service that exposes an MCP server. You're becoming *agentic* with little to no effort. Imagine the possibilities!

Let's talk about some of the possibilities that the MCP opens up for us.

Endless possibilities: know how to prompt, and a world of MCP servers is your oyster

Endless is a big word, so what do we mean? Imagine this: there are skills that you may not have today. In a world with MCP servers, that's no longer a problem, because with APIs wrapped by the MCP, an agent will allow you to prompt to get what you need done.

Take the creation and management of 3D models, for example. **Blender** is a common tool for creating 3D models. To use it, you need 3D modeling skills. So, you will spend hours learning how to use the app, and I'm sure it's a skill worth having.

Due to Blender's MCP server, knowledge of 3D modeling is no longer needed as much. You can instead state what you want done through a prompt. It's like the movie *The Matrix*, where the protagonist, Neo, says, "*I know Kung Fu*" after having information uploaded directly into his brain. The future is here. If you know how to prompt, you're Neo.

Here's the link to the Blender MCP server and the capabilities exposed: `https://github.com/ahujasid/blender-mcp`.

Any client now, with its own LLM and speaking MCP, will be able to call any MCP server, because Blender isn't the only example; other major companies are leaning into MCP as well. Here are some examples:

- GitHub MCP
- Playwright MCP
- Google Maps

For a list of MCP servers, check out the following link: `https://github.com/modelcontextprotocol/servers`.

There are many more servers out there, and more are being added every day, so roll up your sleeves and start building your own MCP servers and use what's out there as well!

You're probably thinking what I'm thinking: we all get our own Jarvis, the AI assistant from the movie Iron Man, capable of doing anything. All we need to do is leverage existing MCP servers and build the ones that are missing; just use MCP.

Imagine having a personal assistant that can help you with anything you need, from scheduling appointments to managing your finances. With MCP, this is now possible.

The future is knocking on your door, loud and clear. Are you ready to answer?

What is the MCP?

Here's what the official MCP website has to say about it:

> *The Model Context Protocol, MCP is an open protocol designed to standardize how applications provide context to* **large language models** *(***LLMs***). Think of it like a USB-C port for AI applications, providing a standardized way to connect AI models to various data sources and tools.*

What does that mean for app developers?

It means the way we build our applications is changing and becoming more standardized. By learning and using MCP, all your apps will be able to communicate with each other and share data in a standardized way. That means you will spend less time worrying about how to connect or *glue* your app to other apps and more time building the features that matter.

We'll dive more into the details of these concepts in the next chapter, but for now, we understand at a mile-high level what the MCP is and how it works, and what major components are involved.

Summary and next steps: now what?

We understand the problem, the solution, and the possibilities, which are endless, and we even know some core concepts of the MCP. But we probably need to know a bit more about it before we can start building our own MCP servers. We'll look at that in the next chapter.

Unlock this book's exclusive benefits now   UNLOCK NOW

Scan this QR code or go to https://packtpub.com/unlock, then search this book by name.

Note: Keep your purchase invoice ready before you start.

2

Explaining the Model Context Protocol

The MCP consists of many parts. In short, **JavaScript Object Notation-Remote Procedure Call (JSON-RPC)** messages are exchanged between the client and the server. A JSON-RPC message is a message following the JSON-RPC specification, which means it has the jsonrpc, id, method, and params fields, and the data type is JSON. An example could look like so:

```
{
  "jsonrpc": "2.0",
  "id": 1,
  "method": "doSomething",
  "params": {
    "foo": "bar"
  }
}
```

💡 **Quick tip**: Enhance your coding experience with the **AI Code Explainer** and **Quick Copy** features. Open this book in the next-gen Packt Reader. Click the **Copy** button

(1) to quickly copy code into your coding environment, or click the **Explain** button

(2) to get the AI assistant to explain a block of code to you.

```
                                                          Copy        Explain
function calculate(a, b) {
    return {sum: a + b};                                   1            2
};
```

📖 **The next-gen Packt Reader** is included for free with the purchase of this book. Scan the QR code OR go to `https://packtpub.com/unlock`, then use the search bar to find this book by name. Double-check the edition shown to make sure you get the right one.

To make it easier to understand, and more interesting, this chapter attempts to explain the protocol by taking you through an implementation of it. For that reason, we hope this chapter is an easier read (not just architecture diagrams) and a glimpse into *how things work*. If you're keen on getting started with building MCP servers, then jump straight to *Chapter 3*, but if you want to understand the MCP protocol a bit more, then keep reading. You can also return to this chapter later.

In this chapter, you will learn about the following:

- The most common message flows in MCP and their message types
- How the underlying SDK implementation roughly works

The chapter covers the following topics:

- Learning about the protocol by implementing it
- Transports in MCP

Learning about the protocol by implementing it

Instead of making this a *dry* chapter about a protocol and its different messages, let's make it enjoyable by actually talking about the processes and messages while implementing them. As part of explaining the process and its flows, you will be shown both the flows as diagrams and also implemented as code. Let's begin.

Transports in MCP

The idea with transports in MCP is that they define how clients and servers communicate. MCP is transport agnostic, meaning it can work over HTTP, WebSockets, STDIO, and more. The transport is the layer that handles the underlying message exchange. It exchanges messages of type JSON-RPC.

MCP has a set of transports it supports from STDIO (for servers running locally) to streamable transports such as WebSockets and **Server-Sent-Events** (**SSEs**), and finally request/response transports such as HTTP.

For each of the specified transports, they all have in common that they operate on streams. All the transports have a method exposing those streams, like so:

```
async with anyio.create_task_group() as tg
    ...
    yield (read_stream, write_stream)
```

There's also a `BaseSession` class that all transports use to send raw JSON-RPC messages, which looks like so.

```
class BaseSession(
    Generic[
        SendRequestT,
        SendNotificationT,
        SendResultT,
        ReceiveRequestT,
```

```
            ReceiveNotificationT,
    ],
):
    ...


def send_request():
    ...


def send_notification():
    ...


def response():
    ...


def _send_response():
    ...
```

This class defines methods such as send_request, send_notification, and response, which send JSON-RPC messages.

STDIO transport

Okay, let's start our journey understanding and implementing the message flow in MCP. We will use the STDIO transport as an example for this exercise. Let's go!

I'm sure you're familiar with seeing messages in the console or even typing into the console – that's **standard input and output**, or **STDIO** for short. But how can we leverage these *streams* for a program? Well, let's start thinking in terms of a server and a client. A client would write a message to a server, and a server would respond with something. Let's look at a very simple server implementation for STDIO:

The server will need to listen to **standard input (stdin)** for incoming messages. In Python, you can use sys.stdin and iterate over it to get the next message, like so:

```
import sys


for line in sys.stdin:
    message = line.strip()
```

We also want to differentiate between simple text messages and JSON-RPC messages. Simple text messages can be handled directly, while JSON-RPC messages will need to be parsed and responded to according to the JSON-RPC specification. Let's identify JSON-RPC messages by their structure with code such as this:

```python
if line.startswith('{"jsonrpc":'):
    json_message = json.loads(line)
    # do something with message
```

Also, we need to send messages back to the calling client. We can do that with `print` and `sys.stdout.flush()`, like so:

```python
print("message")
sys.stdout.flush()
```

Now that we've identified the key elements to implement, let's create the first server:

```python
import sys
import json

while True:
    for line in sys.stdin:
        message = line.strip()
        if message == "hello":
            # send message to client
            print("hello there")
            sys.stdout.flush()  # Ensure output is sent immediately
        elif message.startswith('{"jsonrpc":'):
            # parse it as a JSON message
            json_message = json.loads(message)

            # identify what type of JSON-RPC message it is and
            # respond accordingly
            match json_message['method']:
                case "tools/list":
                    response = {
                        "jsonrpc": "2.0",
                        "id": json_message["id"],
                        "result": ["tool1", "tool2"]
                    }
```

```
                print(json.dumps(response))
                sys.stdout.flush()
                break
          case _:
                print(f"Unknown method: {json_message['method']}")
                sys.stdout.flush()
                break
    elif message == "exit":
        print("Exiting server.")
        sys.stdout.flush()
        sys.exit(0)
    else:
        print(f"Unknown message: {message}")
```

In the preceding code, we've done the following:

- Created code that listens to `sys.stdin`
- Responded with `hello there` if it's being sent `hello` and if given a JSON message, parsed it and thereafter examined its `method` property and responded differently depending on its value
- Added code that makes the program shut down if given the text `exit`

Note how we have code that prints and flushes like so:

```
print(json.dumps(response))
sys.stdout.flush()
```

That can be rewritten as a `send_response` function like so:

```
def send_response(response):
    print(json.dumps(response))
    sys.stdout.flush()
```

This means our server code will now look like so:

```
#server.py
import sys
import json
```

```python
def send_response(response):
    print(json.dumps(response))
    sys.stdout.flush()


while True:
    for line in sys.stdin:
        message = line.strip()
        if message == "hello":
            send_response("hello there")
        elif message.startswith('{"jsonrpc":'):
            json_message = json.loads(message)
            match json_message['method']:
                case "tools/list":
                    response = {
                        "jsonrpc": "2.0",
                        "id": json_message["id"],
                        "result": ["tool1", "tool2"]
                    }
                    send_response(response)
                    break
                case _:
                    send_response(f"Unknown method:
                        {json_message['method']}")
                    break
        elif message == "exit":
            send_response("Exiting server.")
            sys.exit(0)
        else:
            send_response(f"Unknown message: {message}")
```

Creating a client

So, how can we create a client for this? Well, a client should be sending messages and be able to receive server messages. A way to achieve this is by creating the server as a child process with the client being the parent process sending messages to the server. Then, we can communicate with it via standard input and output.

Here's what an implementation can look like:

The way you send a message as a client to the server is by writing to its stdin and reading from its stdout. Here's a simple example:

```
proc.stdin.write(message)
proc.stdin.flush()
```

This code can be refactored to a send_message function like so:

```
def send_message(proc, message):
    proc.stdin.write(message)
    proc.stdin.flush()
```

Let's use the send_message function in our client code when we create the client.

```python
#client.py
import subprocess
import json

# Start the child process
proc = subprocess.Popen(
    ['python3', 'server.py'],  # Replace with your child script
    stdin=subprocess.PIPE,
    stdout=subprocess.PIPE,
    text=True
)

list_tools_message = {
    "jsonrpc": "2.0",
    "id": 1,
    "method": "tools/list",
    "params": {}
};

message = 'hello\n'

def send_message(message):
    """Send a message to the child process."""
    print(f'[CLIENT] Sending message to server...
```

```
        Message: {message.strip()}')
    proc.stdin.write(message)
    proc.stdin.flush()

def serialize_message(message):
    """Serialize a message to JSON format."""
    return json.dumps(message) + '\n'

# Send a message to the child
send_message(message)

# Read response from child
response = proc.stdout.readline()
print('[SERVER]:', response.strip())

# send a JSON-RPC message
send_message(serialize_message(list_tools_message))

response = proc.stdout.readline()
print('[SERVER]:', response.strip())

# this closes down the child process aka server
send_message('exit\n')

proc.stdin.close()
exit_code = proc.wait()
print(f"Child exited with code {exit_code}")
```

Here, you can see how the following happens:

- The client creates a server as a sub-process and ends up writing outgoing messages to said processes via writing to stdin using the send_message method
- Conversely, it listens to stdout for the child process (server) to send back responses with the proc.stdout.readline() code

This code is a great start to build on to start implementing MCP and the STDIO transport. In fact, this is pretty much what happens, except for the fact that MCP communicates with JSON-RPC messages, so let's make it more like MCP next.

MCP and STDIO transport

Our code in the previous section pretty much acted like the STDIO transport does for MCP. For that to be fully true, though, we need the client and server to exchange JSON-RPC messages. So, what are those?

Let's have a look at an example jsonrpc message:

```
const listTools = {
    "jsonrpc": "2.0",
    "id": 1,
    "method": "tools/list",
    "params": {}
};
```

Here, we have a JSON-RPC message, and what makes it one is, first, it's in JSON format, and secondly, it has an attribute called jsonrpc. Furthermore, it should have an id attribute, method, and params. The preceding tools/list message is something a client would send to a server, and the server should respond with its available tools, as this command is used to figure out what tools a server has.

So, what's our first step when building an MCP server? Well, it's the initialization process, also known as a **handshake**, so let's work on that next.

See a running example of this code in the solution folder – check https://github.com/PacktPublishing/Learn-Model-Context-Protocol-with-Python/blob/main/Chapter02/Solutions/README.md.

The initialization process in MCP

Next, now that we have simple client and server code working, we should focus on the initialization process in MCP, sometimes referred to as a handshake.

Here's what initialization looks like at the mile-high level:

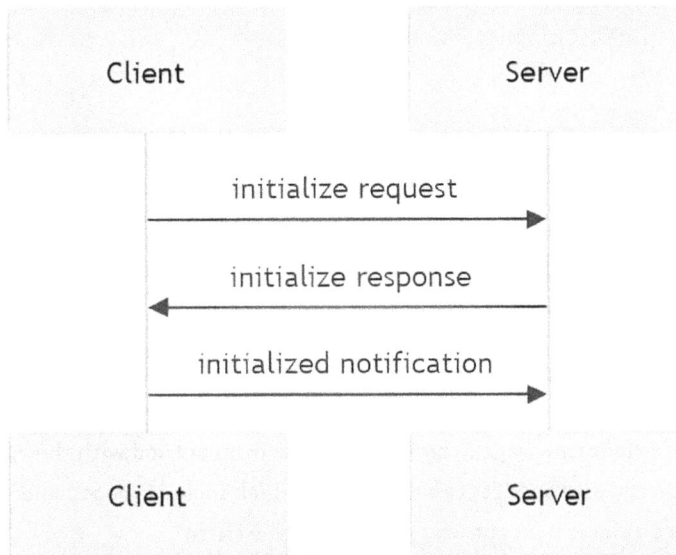

Figure 2.1 – Initialization process

What happens in the preceding process is this:

- First, the client sends an *initialize* request, meaning it wants to know from the server what its capabilities are.
- Then, the server responds with its capabilities – that is, what features it has.
- Lastly, the client lets the server know it's ready to perform operations by sending an *initialized* notification. Before the mentioned notification, any other types of messages, such as listing or running tools, should produce an error response as the *handshake* hasn't fully taken place.

Let's look at the message for each step:

1. **Client sends initialize request**: Here's what the client sends to the server:

```
{
  "jsonrpc": "2.0",
  "id": 1,
  "method": "initialize",
  "params": {
    "protocolVersion": "2024-11-05",
```

```json
    "capabilities": {
      "roots": {
        "listChanged": true
      },
      "sampling": {}
    },
    "clientInfo": {
      "name": "ExampleClient",
      "version": "1.0.0"
    }
  }
}
```

This is an *initialize* message, which you can see from method with the value `initialize`. The client must also send its `capabilities`, which includes `roots` and `sampling` in this case. Here's a closer look at the capabilities of the client:

```json
"capabilities": {
    "roots": {
      "listChanged": true
    },
    "sampling": {}
}
```

2. **Server initializes response**: The server, on the other hand, must answer with a similar message of its capabilities – that is, whether it supports tools, resources, prompts, notifications, and so on. Here's what a typical server response looks like:

```json
{
   "jsonrpc": "2.0",
   "id": 1,
   "result": {
     "protocolVersion": "2024-11-05",
     "capabilities": {
       "logging": {},
       "prompts": {
         "listChanged": true
       },
       "resources": {
```

```
          "subscribe": true,
          "listChanged": true
        },
        "tools": {
          "listChanged": true
        }
      },
      "serverInfo": {
        "name": "ExampleServer",
        "version": "1.0.0"
      }
    }
  }
}
```

Observe the `capabilities` attribute in the response, containing things such as logging, prompts, resources, and tools. **Logging** is the ability of the server to send log messages to the client. We will show an example of logging notifications in *Chapter 5*. The other capabilities – prompts, resources, and tools – are the basic features that a server can have – more on those in *Chapter 3*.

This answer will help the client determine what it can and can't use. It also provides information on protocol version and server info.

Let's have a look at the *initialized* message coming from the client, and then we'll try implementing the preceding message flow.

3. **Concluding the handshake:** As the final step, the client sends an *initialized* message. This is the final message of the *handshake*. Once received, the server is ready to take on any type of JSON-RPC message from the client on tools, resources, or prompts. This message from the client should not produce a response from the server. However, the server should remember it's been initialized. Once initialized, *normal* operations can take place, such as calling tools, prompts, and more. Here's the *initialized* message in detail – as you can see, it doesn't carry much information but is crucial for the client and server to operate normally. Before this notification has been sent, you can't do much.

```
{
  "jsonrpc": "2.0",
  "method": "notifications/initialized"
}
```

How can we implement this? Let us look at that next.

Implementing initialization

There were a few messages exchanged back and forth. In reality, the client can just send `initialized` to the server and you're done, but it's considered good practice to exchange capabilities first via `initialize`.

The client code in the previous subsection was just sending text messages and JSON-RPC messages, but it wasn't really following the flow of the initialization process. To address this, we need to change the client so that it properly handles the initialization sequence. After said sequence is complete, then the client can send other types of messages such as listing tools and so on.

Let's add a connect function to the client and make sure it first asks for server capabilities, followed by notifying the server that things have been initialized.

```python
# client.py

def connect():
    print("Connecting to the server...")
    # 1. Ask for capabilities
    send_message(serialize_message(initialize_message))

    # Read response from child/server
    response = proc.stdout.readline()
    print_response(response, prefix='[SERVER]: \n')

    # 2. Send initialized notification, handshake is done
    send_message(serialize_message(initialized_message))
```

Let's explain the implementation:

- It created a connect function, asking for both capabilities and sending an *initialized* notification.
- It set up a call chain that starts with asking for capabilities by dispatching the *initialize* message, thereafter dispatching *initialized*, and thereby ending the *handshake* process.

Let's improve things further with a `main` function, like so:

```python
def list_tools():
    # 3. send a message to list tools
```

```
    # send a JSON-RPC message
    send_message(serialize_message(list_tools_message))

    response = proc.stdout.readline()
    print_response(response, prefix='[SERVER]: \n')

def close_server():
    send_message('exit\n')

    exit_code = proc.wait()
    print(f"Child exited with code {exit_code}")

def main():
    connect()
    list_tools()
    close_server()

main()
```

Here's what we created:

- We created a main function that connects to the server, lists the tools, and ends up closing the server connection once done
- We defined list_tools, which sends a specific JSON-RPC message that asks the server to list its tools
- Additionally, we created the close_server method, which sends a *quit* message to the server.

Let's work on the server part:

For the server, we need to ensure it reacts accordingly. This means the server needs to only accept messages with an initialize or notifications/initialized method. All other messages before initialization should cause an error. After initialization, all other messages that we support should be okay for the client to send.

To deal with a case of the client trying to do something other than initialization, here's code to handle that:

```
if method != "initialize" and method != "notifications/initialized":
    print(f"Server not initialized. Please send an 'initialized'
```

```
                notification first. You sent {method}")
        sys.stdout.flush()


    continue
```

This code will stop any further processing of the message and wait for the next incoming message.

For the `initialize` and `notifications/initialized` messages, we can handle them like so:

```
match method:
        case "notifications/initialized":
            # print("Server initialized successfully.")
            sys.stdout.flush()
            initialized = True
            break
        case "initialize":
            print(json.dumps(initializeResponse))
            sys.stdout.flush()
            # initialized = True
            break
            # should return capabilities
```

Let's put the code together so we see what the full server looks like:

```
# server.py
# code omitted for brevity

elif message.startswith('{"jsonrpc":'):
  json_message = json.loads(message)
  method = json_message.get('method', '')


  if not initialized:
    if method != "initialize" and method != "notifications/initialized":
        print(f"Server not initialized. Please send an 'initialized'
            notification first. You sent {method}")
      sys.stdout.flush()


      continue


    match method:
```

```
        case "notifications/initialized":
          # print("Server initialized successfully.")
          sys.stdout.flush()
          initialized = True
          break
        case "initialize":
          print(json.dumps(initializeResponse))
          sys.stdout.flush()
          # initialized = True
          break
          # should return capabilities
        case "tools/list":
          response = {
             "jsonrpc": "2.0",
             "id": json_message["id"],
             "result": ["tool1", "tool2"]
          }
          print(json.dumps(response))
          sys.stdout.flush()
          break
        case _:
          print(f"Unknown method: {json_message['method']}")
          sys.stdout.flush()
          break
```

As an exercise, you're recommended to improve the preceding solution as you see fit. You could rewrite this code into a send_response method like so:

```
def send_response(response):
  print(json.dumps(response))
  sys.stdout.flush()
```

In the preceding code, we've done the following:

- Defined an elif that says if we have a JSON-RPC message, we will try to route the message correctly

- Added a check that says, if we're not initialized, and a message is not asking for capabilities or a notification from the client that says "notifications/initialized", then we send a message back indicating this is not an okay message type.

- After initialization, we're okay to accept messages such as listing tools, upon which we respond with our tools in that case.

See a running example of this code in the solution folder. Check *Initialization* (https://github.com/PacktPublishing/Learn-Model-Context-Protocol-with-Python/blob/main/Chapter02/Solutions/README.md).

Supporting features

Now that we have code that's looking more robust, let's support features such as tools, resources, and prompts.

You've already seen how connect is a method we call to handshake with the server. Thereafter, we want to call a tool, a resource, and a prompt, and wait for it to respond before carrying on with the next action. So, for that behavior to be possible, we need to do the following:

1. Place the message on the stream.
2. Wait for the response to arrive.
3. If we get a normal response back, show it, if it's a notification, then ignore it. Notifications from the server are usually a special message or a progress update, and we'll implement support for that in the next section.

Great, we have a plan. Let's revisit our main method to see what we have.

Now, we need to think about what to do with the response from a list_tools() call, like we have in the following code:

```
def main():
    connect()
    list_tools()
    close_server()

main()
```

Ideally, we want to capture the response and do something with that response, such as storing these tools in case we want to call them later via, for example, call_tool (a method that we don't have yet but plan to create).

So, we want the following code to be possible to write:

```
def main():
    connect()
```

```
        tools = list_tools()
        call_tool(tools[0], args) # should specify args to call_tool
        close_server()

    main()
```

At this point, we need to capture the response from `list_tools`, and we need to print it. To make that happen, we need to ensure that both the server and the client are changed. The client needs to store the response in a `tools` variable, and the server needs to recognize that a `list tools` command is being sent and respond with the appropriate JSON-RPC message.

Let's look at the server first. Here, we need to add a new case, `tools/list`, listing all tools:

```
# server.py

# code omitted for brevity

case "tools/list":

    response = {
        "jsonrpc": "2.0",
        "id": json_message["id"],
        "result": {
            "tools": [
                {
                    "name": "example_tool",
                    "description": "An example tool that does something.",
                    "inputSchema": {
                        "type": "object",
                        "properties": {
                            "arg1": {
                                "type": "string",
                                "description": "An example argument."
                            }
                        },
                        "required": ["arg1"]
                    }
                }
            ]
```

```
        }
    }
    print(json.dumps(response))
    sys.stdout.flush()
    break
```

What's worth calling out in the preceding code is the following:

- The `tools` property: This should point to a list of tools.
- `inputSchema`: This schema should describe the parameters this tool accepts and whether they're mandatory to send. For this specific tool, it's called `example_tool` and it has one parameter, `arg1`, which is required.

Now that we have the server side done, let's focus on the client next. First, let's define the `list_tools` method:

```
# client.py

def list_tools():
    # 3. send a message to list tools
    # send a JSON-RPC message
    send_message(serialize_message(list_tools_message))
    response = proc.stdout.readline()
    return json.loads(response)['result']['tools']
```

Next, let's use `list_tools` from the main method:

```
# client.py

tools = []

def main():
    connect()
    tool_response = list_tools()
    tools.extend(tool_response)

    print("Tools available:", tools)
```

In the main method, we call `list_tools`, save the `tool_response` response, and add it to a `tools` list that we will use later when we try calling one of the tools on the server.

We also need to support how to call a tool. Like before, let's add the server part first:

```python
# server.py

case "tools/call":
    tool_name = json_message['params']['name']
    args = json_message['params']['args']
    # todo create a response for the tool call, i.e call the right tool
    response = {
        "jsonrpc": "2.0",
        "id": json_message["id"],
        "result": {
            "properties": {
                "content": {
                    "description": "description of the content",
                    "items": [
                        { "type": "text", "text": f"Called tool
                            {tool_name} with arguments {args}" }
                    ]
                }
            }
        }
    }
    print(json.dumps(response))
    sys.stdout.flush()
    break
```

In the preceding code, we've done the following:

- Constructed a message in a JSON-RPC message.

- Added result with the properties attribute, which itself has an attribute, content. Said property has an items array that contains a number of text blocks describing the outcome of calling the tool. In a more real implementation, the tool in question should be called, and its result should be listed here.

Let's focus on the client part next. We need a `call_tool` method:

```python
# omitting code for brevity

def call_tool(tool_name, args):
    # 4. call a tool
    # send a JSON-RPC message
    tool_message = {
        "jsonrpc": "2.0",
        "method": "tools/call",
        "params": {
            "name": tool_name,
            "args": args
        },
        "id": 1
    }
    send_message(serialize_message(tool_message))
    response = proc.stdout.readline()
    return
        json.loads(response)["result"]["properties"]["content"]["items"]
```

Here, we do the following:

- Construct a JSON-RPC message, and we pass in `tool_name` and `args` as part of the message.
- Handle the response by loading it as JSON and dive into the response to fetch out `items`, which contains the relevant part of the response.

In the `main` method, we need to add the following code:

```python
def main():
    connect()
    tool_response = list_tools()
    tools.extend(tool_response)

    print("Tools available:", tools)

    tool = tools[0]
```

```
    tool_call_response = call_tool(tool["name"],{"args1": "hello"})
    for content in tool_call_response:
        print_response(content['text'], prefix='[SERVER] tool response: \n')
    # print_response(tool_call_response['result'], prefix='[SERVER]: \n')

    # call tool, we need a name and arguments
    close_server()
```

In the preceding code, we've done the following:

- Called call_tool with the name of the tool, and we also passed arguments. We hardcoded the arguments.
- Iterated over the response to get the text block response we defined on the server.

With all these parts in place, running the program should now also list this as part of the output:

```
[CLIENT]: {
  "jsonrpc": "2.0",
  "method": "tools/call",
  "params": {
    "name": "example_tool",
    "args": {
      "arg1": {
        "type": "string",
        "description": "An example argument."
      }
    }
  },
  "id": 1
}
[SERVER] tool response:
 Called tool example_tool with arguments {'args1': 'hello'}
```

Great, now we have the features we need to both list the tools on the server and call a tool. It should be said, though, that calling a tool should also perform a computation. At present, we just list what tool was called and with what argument, so it's a good start, but we should improve this further.

Let's move on to notifications next. Notifications can be sent in both directions, from server to client as well as from client to server.

See a running example of this code in the solution folder – check *Features* (`https://github.com/
PacktPublishing/Learn-Model-Context-Protocol-with-Python/blob/main/Chapter02/
Solutions/README.md`).

Notifications, report progress, and important updates

Notifications are something both the client and the server can send to each other. Usually, they
want to tell each party something important happened – for example, a long-running tool response
might report progress, or a server may send a message to report on a change in its capabilities.
So, how can we support notifications? Well, there are two aspects of it:

- **Sending a notification-type message** from either client or server. This looks like so:

```
{
    "jsonrpc": "2.0",
    "method": "notifications/[type]",
    "params": {}
}
```

  `[type]` is usually `cancelled` or `progress`. For a full specification of types, check
  `https://github.com/modelcontextprotocol/modelcontextprotocol/blob/main/
  schema/2025-03-26/schema.ts`.

- **The role of the notification**. For a client, a notification is seen as an extra thing, and something you should show, for example, in a user interface to improve the user's experience.
  A notification from a client to a server, though, tends to be different. For example, a client
  sends a notification to the server to set the state to `"initialized"`.

How can we implement this, then? Well, we mostly have it in place already. We're going to add
the following to our code, though:

- Dispatch a notification from the server to, in this case, report progress while waiting for
  the result of calling a tool

- Add logic to our `list_tools` and `call_tool` functions to support handling an arriving
  notification.

First, let's see how we can support notifications on the client:

```
# client.py
# code omitted for brevity
```

```
def list_tools():
    # 3. send a message to list tools
    # send a JSON-RPC message
    send_message(serialize_message(list_tools_message))

    has_result = False
    while not has_result:
        response = proc.stdout.readline()
        # check if message has result attribute, if so break out of loop

        parsed_response = json.loads(response)
        if 'result' in parsed_response:
            has_result = True
            return parsed_response['result']['tools']
        else:
            # this is a notification, we can print it
            print_response(response, prefix='[SERVER] notification: \n')
```

Here, we have rewritten `list_tools` and added a loop to it. As long as what we receive is not the final result, we print it out (as it's a notification). Then, once we get the final result – that is, it contains a `result` property – we return it from the function.

How can we deal with this on the server side? There are a few things we need:

- A notification message needs to be created. We can place that in our `utils` folder and `messages.py`.

```
# utils/messages.py

progress_notification = {
    "jsonrpc": "2.0",
    "method": "notifications/progress",
    "params": {
        "message": "Working on it..."
    }
};
```

- We need to dispatch the actual notification from where we want it to happen. For the sake of showing how it works, let's add it to the `tools/list` case like so:

```python
# server.py
# code omitted for brevity
case "tools/list":
    # send notification about progress first, then later the
    #response
    print(json.dumps(progress_notification))
    sys.stdout.flush()
```

It should be said that progress notifications, in particular, should be used when calling tools, rather than listing what tools you have, as calling a tool might be a lengthy operation in some cases, so let's add that next. First, let's redo `call_tool` in the same way as `list_tools` on the client:

```python
# client.py
# code omitted for brevity

def call_tool(tool_name, args):
    # 4. call a tool
    # send a JSON-RPC message

    tool_message = {
        "jsonrpc": "2.0",
        "method": "tools/call",
        "params": {
            "name": tool_name,
            "args": args
        },
        "id": 1
    }

    has_result = False
    send_message(serialize_message(tool_message))

    while not has_result:
        response = proc.stdout.readline()
        parsed_response = json.loads(response)
```

```
            if 'result' in parsed_response:
                has_result = True
                return
                    parsed_response["result"]["properties"]
                        ["content"]["items"]
            else:
                # this is a notification, we can print it
                print_response(response, prefix='[SERVER]
                    notification: \n')
```

Just like with `list_tools`, we add a loop that just prints notifications unless the final result shows up. There's definitely some duplication of code here, so we might want to break that out into a utility function at some point. Let's see what we need to add on the server:

```
# server.py
# code omitted for brevity

case "tools/call":
    tool_name = json_message['params']['name']
    args = json_message['params']['args']

    print(json.dumps(progress_notification))
    sys.stdout.flush()

    print(json.dumps(progress_notification))
    sys.stdout.flush()
```

Okay, so now we've added code that sends two notifications to the case that takes care of incoming messages of type `tools/call`.

When we try to run it all again, we should now see the following at the end of the output:

```
[SERVER] notification:
 {
  "jsonrpc": "2.0",
  "method": "notifications/progress",
  "params": {
    "message": "Working on it..."
  }
 }
```

```
[SERVER] notification:
 {
  "jsonrpc": "2.0",
  "method": "notifications/progress",
  "params": {
    "message": "Working on it..."
  }
 }
[SERVER] tool response:
 Called tool example_tool with arguments {'args1': 'hello'}
```

Clearly, the two notifications arrive before the tool calling response.

It should be said, from a performance standpoint, that where we treat this as an SDK implementation, we would probably change and add the asyncio library to ensure we're non-blocking. For the sake of demonstrating how messages flow back and forth, it serves its purpose, but it could be improved a bit.

Great – we've managed to implement notifications and did some nice refactoring. Let's look at sampling next.

See a running example of this code in the solution folder – check *Notifications* (https://github. com/PacktPublishing/Learn-Model-Context-Protocol-with-Python/blob/main/Chapter02/ Solutions/README.md).

Sampling – help the server complete a request

Sampling is an interesting feature. What it means is that the server is telling the client, *I don't know how to do this*, or *You do it better – can you please help me complete this request?*. More specifically, the server asks the client to complete the request using the client's **large language model** (**LLM**).

Okay, so we established that the server sometimes needs the client to help it complete a request. The way the client helps is by asking its LLM for the response, which it then passes back to the server.

What is the starting point, though? Well, it could be a client that calls a tool on the server, and then the tool generates a sampling request. Then the flow could look like so:

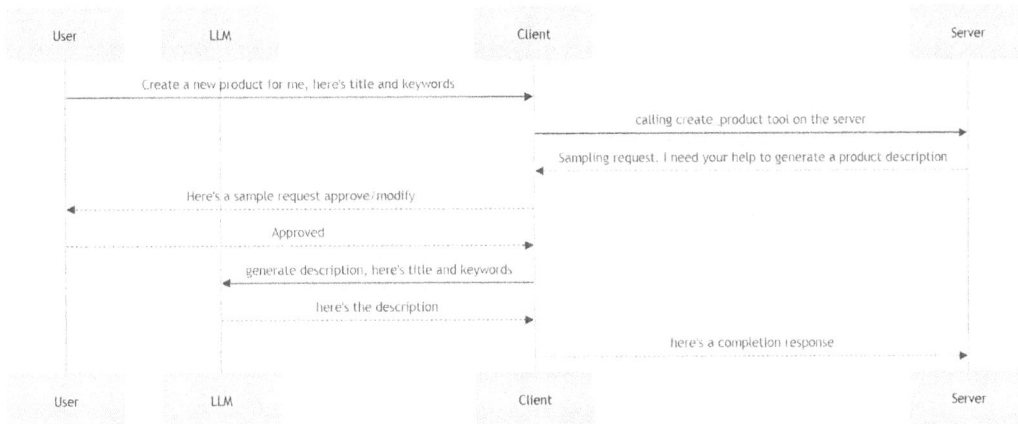

Figure 2.2 – Sampling flow, scenario 1

🔍**Quick tip**: Need to see a high-resolution version of this image? Open this book in the next-gen Packt Reader or view it in the PDF/ePub copy.

📖**The next-gen Packt Reader** and a **free PDF/ePub copy** of this book are included with your purchase. Scan the QR code OR visit https://packtpub.com/unlock, then use the search bar to find this book by name. Double-check the edition shown to make sure you get the right one.

Or, it could be an external service that generates an event that the server listens to. Here's the flow for that scenario:

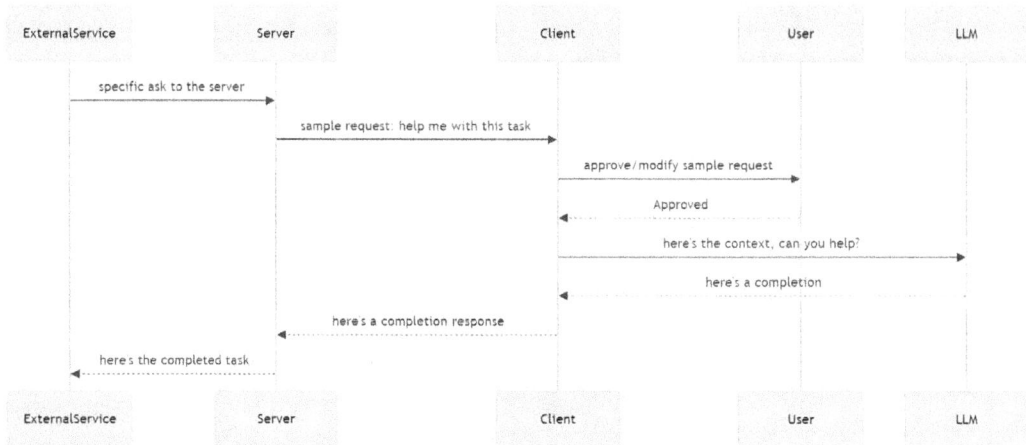

Figure 2.3 – Sampling flow, scenario 2

From a message standpoint, here's what the server is sending to the client:

```
{
  messages: [
    {
      role: "user" | "assistant",
      content: {
        type: "text" | "image",

        // For text:
        text?: string,

        // For images:
        data?: string,              // base64 encoded
        mimeType?: string
      }
    }
  ],
  modelPreferences?: {
    hints?: [{
      name?: string                 // Suggested model name/family
```

```
    }],
    costPriority?: number,        // 0-1, importance of minimizing cost
    speedPriority?: number,       // 0-1, importance of low latency
    intelligencePriority?: number // 0-1, importance of capabilities
  },
  systemPrompt?: string,
  includeContext?: "none" | "thisServer" | "allServers",
  temperature?: number,
  maxTokens: number,
  stopSequences?: string[],
  metadata?: Record<string, unknown>
}
```

Here's some of the information included in the preceding request:

- messages is a chat conversation between an assistant and a user, and provides the required context for the request

- modelPreferences: Here, the server can specify things such as the preferred model name and decide the prioritization of cost, speed, and capabilities

There's also model configuration data being sent on temperature, the number of tokens to use, and more. It's worth calling out that these are recommendations that the client can choose to accept or modify.

The client should then respond with a completion message, like so:

```
{
  model: string,   // Name of the model used
  stopReason?: "endTurn" | "stopSequence" | "maxTokens" | string,
  role: "user" | "assistant",
  content: {
    type: "text" | "image",
    text?: string,
    data?: string,
    mimeType?: string
  }
}
```

In the preceding response, the following information is covered:

- `model` is the model used. It doesn't have to be the same as what the server asked for.

- `stopReason` – it's good to know whether you got a full response or whether it stopped for some other reason.

- `content` is the content response.

Introducing a scenario: e-commerce

When does this happen, though? Well, the server could be listening to events that it should react to. For example, let's say you have an e-commerce scenario and there are new products being registered by a system somewhere. However, before these products can be sold, they need a proper description. This description is something a client and its LLM can help with.

Figure 2.4 – E-commerce scenario flow

In the final step, the server logs, stores, and possibly caches the response.

Let's look at a request in this context. Here's an example request from a server:

```
{
  "method": "sampling/createMessage",
  "params": {
    "messages": [
      {
        "role": "user",
        "content": {
          "type": "text",
          "text": "Create a selling product description for this sweater,
```

```
                    keywords autumn, cozy, knitted"
        }
      }
    ],
    "systemPrompt": "You are a helpful assistant assisting with
      product descriptions",
    "includeContext": "thisServer",
    "maxTokens": 300
  }
}
```

As you can see, we settled on only providing it with context and omitted any recommendations on the model to use or configuration, but we could add that if we wanted.

It's now up to the client how to interpret this request and respond.

Implementing sampling

Let's implement sampling in our code, and we'll use the product description scenario so you can see how it can be used. Here's what we need:

- **External service**: This service should produce a new product in need of a product description. This product has been registered by someone else in another system and shows up in this server as a message payload as a result of listening to an event. This is scenario-specific code.
- **Server – sample request**: We just need the capability to send a `json-rpc` request.
- **Client response**: We need to listen to this specific message type, call the LLM using the message's payload, and return a response to the server.

Let's start with the external service. This isn't really part of MCP, but it will hopefully give you a sense of how you can integrate an external component that produces a message that you're interested in:

Here, we are adding the external service that will end up registering new products. It will produce new products at random intervals and send them to any listener.

```python
# server.py
# code omitted for brevity

class ProductStore:
    def __init__(self):
```

```python
        self.started = False
        self.listeners = {}
        # create timer that adds a product to the queue every 5 seconds

    def add_product(self):
        """Add a product to the store and notify listeners."""
        product = {
            "id": str(random.randint(10000, 99999)),
            "name": f"Product {random.randint(1, 100)}",
            "price": round(random.uniform(10.0, 100.0), 2),
            "keywords": [f"keyword{random.randint(1, 5)}" for _ in
                range(random.randint(1, 3))]
        }
        self.dispatch_message("new_product", product)

    def start_product_queue_timer(self):
        """Start a timer that adds a product to the queue
            every 5 seconds."""
        def schedule_next():
            delay = random.uniform(1, 2)
            self.product_timer = threading.Timer(delay, self.add_product)
            self.product_timer.start()

        def add_twice():
            schedule_next()
            schedule_next()

        add_twice()

    def add_listener(self, message, callback):
        if not self.started:
            self.started = True
            self.start_product_queue_timer()
        """Add a listener for product updates."""
        # In a real application, this would register the callback
        #to be called when a new product is added
        callbacks = self.listeners.get(message, [])
```

```
        callbacks.append(callback)
        self.listeners[message] = callbacks


    def dispatch_message(self, message, payload):
        """Dispatch a message to all registered listeners."""
        callbacks = self.listeners.get(message, [])
        for callback in callbacks:
            callback(payload)
```

First, we create a class capable of creating and dispatching products that we want the client's help with. In the previously mentioned scenario, we needed the client and its LLM to produce a description for us.

Here's what the product store code consists of:

- A `ProductStore` class: This store should emulate an external source that raises events that, at any point, can send new products that need their product descriptions augmented. See the store as a queue that could, for example, be long-polling an API or listening to a message queue. The point is it's just a placeholder and only you know what this construct is as it's solution-specific.

- Several helper methods, such as `add_listener`, `dispatch_message`, and `start_product_queue_timer`: The latter is responsible for starting a timer for dispatching the products at a certain time interval.

Now we will interact with the product store by first creating it and then adding a listener to it. The listener should dispatch a message to the client whenever a new product is added.

```
def create_sampling_message(product):
    sampling_message = {
        "jsonrpc": "2.0",
        "id": 1,
        "method": "sampling/createMessage",
        "params": {
            "messages": [{
                "role": "system",
                "content": {
                    "type": "text",
                    "text": f"New product available:
                        {product['name']} (ID: {product['id']},
```

```
                                  Price: {product['price']}). Keywords:
                                  {', '.join(product['keywords'])}"
                }
            }],
            "systemPrompt": "You are a helpful assistant assisting
                with product descriptions",
            "includeContext": "thisServer",
            "maxTokens": 300
        }
    }
    return sampling_message


store = ProductStore()
store.add_listener("new_product", lambda product:
    print(json.dumps(create_sampling_message(product))))
```

We also need a way on the server to receive a sampling response from the client. Let's see how we can handle that next. The main problem we have with the client is that we're not really set up to handle a message that can arrive at any time. What we have right now is that we explicitly send calls from the client to the server and expect a response that we handle. To address this, we need to change our architecture slightly to use a background thread. That works in the following way:

1. The thread listens to messages on `stdout`.

2. If a message arrives (sent from the server), then it will be put in a queue for later processing.

3. For sample messages, we will not put those in a queue but handle them directly, and for notifications and normal responses, we will have them in a queue and let them be handled in their respective method (e.g., `list_tools`, `call_tool`, etc.).

Let's show how we set up the thread next:

```
# client.py


def listen_to_stdout():
    """Listen to the stdout of the child process and handle messages."""
    while True:
        response = proc.stdout.readline()
        if not response:
            break  # Exit if no more output
```

```
        try:
            parsed_response = json.loads(response)
            if is_sampling_message(parsed_response):
                handle_sampling_message(parsed_response)
                # consume message if it is a sampling message
            else:
                # put message in the queue for further processing
                message_queue.put(response.strip())
        except json.JSONDecodeError:
            # If the response is not JSON, just print it
            print("[THREAD] Non-JSON response received:",
                response.strip())
            # print_response(response, prefix='[THREAD]: \n')


# create thread and start it
listener_thread = threading.Thread(target=listen_to_stdout, daemon=True)
listener_thread.start()
```

The preceding code does the following:

- Reads from stdout.

- Checks to see whether there's a sampling message. If so, it tries to handle it by calling handle_sampling_message. If it's not a sampling message, then it's put in the queue.

Here are some helper methods that we also need:

```
def is_sampling_message(message):
    """Check if a message is a sampling message."""
    return message.get('method', '').startswith('sampling')


def create_sampling_message(llm_response):
    """Create a sampling message for a product."""
    sampling_message = {
        "jsonrpc": "2.0",
        "result": {
            "content": {
                "text": llm_response
            }
        }
```

```
    }
    return sampling_message


def call_llm(message):
    return "LLM: " + message



def handle_sampling_message(message):
    """Handle a sampling message."""
    print("[CLIENT] Calling LLM to complete request", message)
    # get content info from message, send that to LLM

    content = message['params']['messages'][0]['content']['text']
    llm_response = call_llm(content)
    message = create_sampling_message(llm_response)
    send_message(serialize_message(message))
    # should call LLM to complete request
```

Especially of interest is `handle_sampling_message`, which takes the message from the server and calls `call_llm` (we stubbed out this method; you should ensure in a real implementation that it calls an actual LLM). Then the response is constructed and sent back to the server for caching, logging, or whatever else the server needs to do with it.

Because we now rely on this queue for messages, we need to alter `list_tools` and `call_tool` to read from this queue instead of reading from the stream, like so:

```
while not has_result:
    # response = proc.stdout.readline()
    response = message_queue.get()
```

Here, we have commented how we used to ask for the latest message, calling `readline`, and we now instead call `message_queue.get`.

That's it – that's how sampling works. It originates in the server as the result of an event, and then it asks the client for help, and the client responds. It should be emphasized that the client doesn't have to do exactly what the server wants it to do – that is, use a specific mode or configuration. You should present the server request in front of an equal user so they have a chance to respond and configure what the client sends back – that is, *human in the loop*.

See a running example of this code in the solution folder – check *Sampling* (`https://github.com/ PacktPublishing/Learn-Model-Context-Protocol-with-Python/blob/main/Chapter02/ Solutions/README.md`).

SSE transport

At this point, we've gone through large parts of the MCP. So, what's the difference between SSE and STDIO? The main difference is how messages flow. In STDIO, messages are passed on your local machine between `stdin` and `stdout` streams; for SSE, messages flow over the web using HTTP. That means all the major motions, such as handshake, initialization, tool calling, and so on, need to be rethought as web requests from the client and web requests to the server.

Conceptually, SSE transport is implemented as a web server with the `/messages` and `/sse` routes. The former handles incoming MCP messages, while the latter is used to establish a connection for streaming events.

Here's what that looks like from a high level:

Figure 2.5 – SSE transport flow

We will cover SSE in more detail in *Chapter 4*, but now we have a good understanding at a mile-high level of what the difference is compared to STDIO.

Streamable HTTP

Streamable HTTP is just like SSE in the sense that MCP servers using Streamable HTTP can be reached via a URL on the web. There are some differences and similarities. Let's make that a bit clearer:

- Both SSE and Streamable HTTP need the client to accept text/event-stream. For Streamable HTTP, the client also needs to accept application/json, as the server can choose whether to stream responses or send them as JSON. For SSE, the server always sends content as text/event-stream.
- SSE connections are usually long-lived GET requests, where Streamable HTTP is typically POST.

From an implementation standpoint, it's very similar to that of SSE – that is, it's implemented as a web server. However, for Streamable HTTP, in the context of MCP, you should set up a route, /mcp, that handles both connections and messages, and it should also be set up as POST.

Client		Server
	POST /mcp { JSON-RPC initialize } →	
	← { JSON-RPC response initialize} /mcp?sessionId=<sessionId>	
	/mcp, { JSON-RPC payload initialized }, handshake done →	
	/mcp, { JSON-RPC payload any request e.g listTools, callTool } →	
	← JSON-RPC response	
Client		Server

Figure 2.6 – Streamable HTTP flow

Therefore, implementing Streamable HTTP is a bit easier than SSE as you only need to keep track of one endpoint, /mcp. There's more on Streamable HTTP in *Chapter 5*.

Summary

In this chapter, we covered quite a bit of information. The most important takeaway is that client and server communication needs to be initialized before further action can take place. Fortunately, most SDKs take care of the initialization part, and you can usually start the client-server communication by calling and listing tools and more. Hopefully, this was a good read for both those who find diagrams clarifying and those who like to see how code looks. The code *works*, but could surely be improved for performance, maintainability, and more. Do give the code a try – check the solutions folder.

In the next chapter, we will learn how to build and test our first server. The chapter will serve as a good introduction to getting hands-on with MCP.

Assignment

Try running the code provided in https://github.com/PacktPublishing/Learn-Model-Context-Protocol-with-Python/blob/main/Chapter02/Solutions/README.md to see how things work. The code should do the following:

- Initialize a connection
- Send an initialized notification
- List tools
- Call a tool and produce notifications
- Produce sample messages

The code is built up in steps, so it's worth going through all the subfolders for your chosen runtime.

Solution

You can access the solution at https://github.com/PacktPublishing/Learn-Model-Context-Protocol-with-Python/blob/main/Chapter02/Solutions/README.md.

Quiz

What needs to happen before a *handshake* between a server and a client can be considered complete?

- A: The client needs to first send *initialize*, wait for the server response, and then send *initialized*.

- B: The client and server can call, for example, list tools right away.

- C: The client needs to send *initialized* to the server.

You can access the solution at `https://github.com/PacktPublishing/Learn-Model-Context-Protocol-with-Python/blob/main/Chapter02/Solutions/solution-quiz.md`.

Unlock this book's exclusive benefits now

UNLOCK NOW

Scan this QR code or go to `https://packtpub.com/unlock`, then search this book by name.

Note: Keep your purchase invoice ready before you start.

3

Building and Testing Servers

In this chapter, we will cover the basics of building and testing servers. We will start with a simple server that uses the STDIO transport. The STDIO transport is a simple way to communicate with the server using standard input and output streams. Building STDIO servers is a great way to get started with the **Model Context Protocol (MCP)** and understand how it works. It should also be added that the STDIO transport is the most common way to communicate with the server, and it's meant for servers running on your machine.

As part of the chapter, we will also cover different ways of testing the server. It's important that what we build works as expected. We will cover different tools that can be used visually, in the CLI, and in code.

In this chapter, you will learn how to do the following:

- Build a simple server using the STDIO transport
- Describe the core concepts of the server
- Test the server using different tools

The chapter covers the following topics:

- A STDIO server
- Concepts
- Runtimes
- Testing the server
- First server

A STDIO server

Using STDIO transport means that the server communicates with the client through standard input and output streams. This means that the server can read input from the client via **standard input (stdin)** and send output back to the client via **standard output (stdout)**. Okay, that sounds simple, but how does it work?

MCP uses JSON-RPC 2.0 as its wire format. Thereby, it needs to convert stream messages into JSON-RPC format for transmission and convert received JSON-RPC messages back into stream messages. Imagine the following example in the terminal:

```
>> hello world
```

To be used in a STDIO server, the preceding message would be converted into JSON-RPC format, and it would look like this:

```
{
    "jsonrpc": "2.0",
    "method": "sendMessage",
    "params": {
      "message": "hello world"
    },
    "id": 1
}
```

That's an interesting example, but what really matters to you as a developer is two things:

- How to build a STDIO server. We'll show this shortly in an upcoming section.
- Why it matters, and what it means that your server is a STDIO server. It means that your server is running on your local machine and is communicating with the client through standard input and output streams. In *Chapter 4* and *Chapter 5*, we'll show you how to build a server that can communicate with servers over the internet.

Concepts

Let's take a look at the core concepts (features, if you will) that the server can offer.

Resources

These are the data and context that the server can provide to the client. The way MCP is meant to be used is by the client having an LLM when they communicate with the server. Resources in this use case serve as context that could be added to the LLM at the time of the prompt. Imagine the following scenario playing out:

Figure 3.1 – Resources scenario

In this scenario, the context ensures that the end user gets a better result as the server's context is paired with the user's prompt, like a simplified **retrieval-augmented generation (RAG)** pattern. That is, you pair the user's prompt with your data to get a better response.

A specific example implementing this way of thinking could be where the user asks for products like so:

Prompt

```
User: I'm looking for a new laptop
```

Figure 3.2 – Example of a resource interaction

In this specific product query, we call resources first to learn what table to query, and then we let the LLM identify which tool to call. Thanks to calling the resource, we gain extra knowledge on what tools to select and what parameters to use.

Resources can also be used in a manner where the LLM isn't used, but the way you should think about your server is that it's here to empower a client's LLM. That means the tools, resources, and prompts you provide should be helpful.

Now that we understand when resources are used, let's talk more about the nature of them. Resources are static and can be anything that the server can access and share with the client. What's important to know is that you can ask for a resource either with or without a template. If there's only one file or one app setting configuration, it makes sense to create that with a set name such as config:

```
server.resource(
  "config",
  "config://app",
  async (uri) => ({
    contents: [{
      uri: uri.href,
```

```
        text: "App configuration here"
    }]
  })
);
```

Here, we are returning the same type of information each time.

However, if there are many types of settings, such as user settings, calendar settings, and so on, it might make sense to create a more templated version such as `settings://{type}`:

```
@mcp.resource("settings://{type}")
def get_setting(type: str) -> str:
    """Get a specific setting"""
    return f"Setting from file {type}!"
```

The settings are still non-changing, but there are many of them, so we choose to group them under one namespace.

In this case, the resource is called `settings` and takes type as a parameter. For example, `settings://hello` would match this pattern.

Tools

Tools are the functions or capabilities that the server can perform. Examples of tools include data processing functions, tools that call an API to fetch data, and more. For tools, we need to define the input and output by providing a schema. How this is done looks different depending on the used runtime, but the idea is that it should be clear to the consumer of the tool what the input and output are. For example, if we have a tool that takes two numbers and returns their product, we can define it like this:

```
# Add a multiplication tool
@mcp.tool()
def multiply(a: int, b: int) -> int:
    """Multiply two numbers"""
    return a * b
```

In this example, we define a tool called `multiply` that takes two numbers as input and returns their product. The input and output are defined using Python type hints.

Prompts

Prompts are the templated messages or workflows that guide the interactions between the client and server. A good example of a prompt is a template that helps the client write a product description or slogan in the context of an e-commerce application. Just like resources and tools, prompts can take input. Here's an example of a prompt that takes a product name and returns a product description:

```
@mcp.prompt()
def describe_product(product: str) -> str:
    return f"Write a product description for {product}"
```

Here, we define a prompt called `describe_product` that takes a product name as input and returns a product description. The input is defined using Python type hints.

Now that we know what our server can contain, what else do we need to know?

Runtimes

The officially supported runtimes at present for MCP are TypeScript, Python, .NET, Java and Kotlin, Rust, and Go. More are being added all the time. For an updated list of runtimes, please refer to the MCP documentation here: `https://modelcontextprotocol.io/docs/sdk`. Each of these runtimes has its own SDK you can use. The implementation of the runtimes is similar, but there are some differences.

Excited? Let's get started!

Testing the server

There are many tools at your disposal to test the server. Why we test is that we want to ensure that the server is working as expected. The tools we will cover in this chapter are as follows.

Inspector

This is a CLI tool that can present both a UI and a CLI interface. The latter is meant for scripting and automation.

> The inspector tool runs a Node.js package with npx, so ensure that you have the Node.js runtime installed. This is also true even if you run the inspector tool via a Python command, as Python wraps a call to the underlying Node.js process.

The UI is meant for manual testing and debugging. In this example command, we run the inspector tool. Ensure that you stand in the same directory as the server file when you run the following commands.

The Python SDK installed an executable mcp that helps run the server:

```
mcp dev server.py
```

By running this tool, we can test the server in visual mode. Here's a screenshot of the inspector tool:

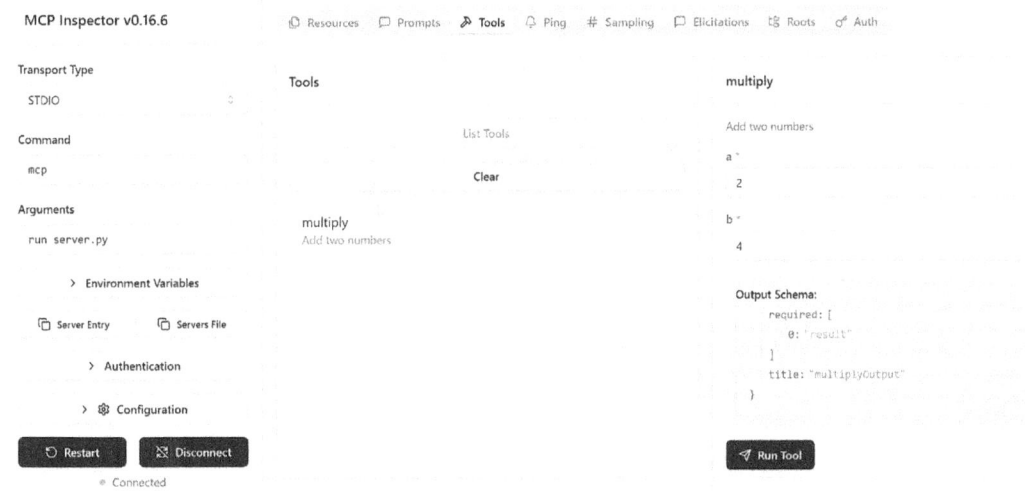

Figure 3.3 – Inspector tool

Ensure that the visual tool specifies the following fields:

- **Transport Type: STDIO**
- **Command:** mcp
- **Arguments:** run server.py

You can also run the inspector tool in CLI mode. This is useful for scripting and automation. You type almost the same command as earlier, but you add the --cli flag:

```
npx @modelcontextprotocol/inspector --cli mcp run server.py --method
tools/list
```

Here, we are adding the --method command followed by the tools/list argument, which says we want to list all tools on the server.

Note that mcp dev in the Python pivot earlier wraps a Node.js tool, which is the inspector. If you want full access to all the features of the inspector, you can run it directly for both Node.js and Python, and that's what we recommend doing (that is, run it like so: npx @modelcontextprotocol/inspector).

cURL

A standard command-line tool such as cURL can be used to send requests to the server. This is normally used to test servers using SSE or streamable HTTP as transport. Other tools capable of making web requests can be used as well. A curl command will only work if the server is running on the internet, which is the case with SSE servers. For STDIO servers, you need to use the inspector or a custom client to send requests to the server. Let's see a typical curl command:

```
curl -X POST -H "Content-Type: application/json" -d '{"method": "tools/list", "params": {}, "id": 1}' http://localhost:3000/sse
```

In the preceding command, we are sending a POST request to the server with the tools/list method. The server will respond with a list of tools available on the server. This is a good alternative to using the inspector in CLI mode.

Tests

It's possible to write unit tests for the server. This is a good practice in addition to using the inspector. The tests can be run in a CI/CD pipeline and are useful to ensure that the server is working as expected. You can use any testing framework you like, and you can add resources, tools, and prompts to the server and then test them. Let's see an example of a test:

```python
@pytest.mark.anyio
async def test_add_tool_decorator(self):
    mcp = FastMCP()

    @mcp.tool()
    def add(x: int, y: int) -> int:
        return x + y

    assert len(mcp._tool_manager.list_tools()) == 1
```

In the preceding example, we do the following:

- Use the pytest framework to test the server
- Create a new server instance and add a tool called add
- Test that the tool is added to the server and that the number of tools is equal to 1

This is a simple test, but it shows how you can use pytest to test the server.

Now, we have a good grasp of the concepts and features of the server; let's write down the plan for how we will go about building our first server.

First server

To build our first server, let's first go through the steps to build a simple server:

1. **Create a new project**: We will create a new project with the needed dependencies and set up any environment specifics. You're highly encouraged to create a virtual environment to ensure you don't install libraries globally. By using a virtual environment, each project is isolated from other projects and you don't have to worry about conflicting library versions that might otherwise occur.

2. **Install dependencies**: Here, we will list and install dependencies for the project, which differ, of course, depending on the runtime you are using.

3. **Add server code**: This is where we will add the server's features. As part of this, we will discuss the feature, its input and output, and schemas.

4. **Test the server with inspector**: Inspector is a tool that helps you ensure new features work okay. The tool allows you to run it in both CLI mode and a visual mode, where it shows a web browser UI:

   - The CLI mode is appropriate for CI/CD scenarios, as it responds with JSON in a terminal
   - The visual mode is more appropriate when you, as a developer, try to ensure that the server is working as it should

Let's write some code!

Step 1: Create a new project

Before we write any code, we need a project. This will set us up for success. The project will contain everything we need to write our server and define tests and scripts for testing and running the server:

1. Create the following folder structure:

    ```
    ├── src/
    |---- server.py
    ```

2. Create a virtual environment:

    ```
    python -m venv venv
    ```

3. Activate the virtual environment:

    ```
    venv\Scripts\activate
    ```

    You should see the name of the virtual environment in the terminal prompt. This means that the virtual environment is activated, and any packages you install will be installed in this environment.

Great, now we have a virtual environment and a folder structure. Next, we need to install the dependencies.

Step 2: Install dependencies

Run the following command in the terminal:

```
pip install "mcp[cli]"
```

This will install the MCP SDK and the CLI tools.

Step 3: Add server code

Add the following code to server.py:

```
# server.py
from mcp.server.fastmcp import FastMCP


# Create an MCP server
```

```
mcp = FastMCP("Demo")


# Add a multiply tool
@mcp.tool()
def multiply(first: int, second: int) -> int:
    """Multiply two numbers"""
    return first * second


# Add a dynamic greeting resource
@mcp.resource("greeting://{name}")
def get_greeting(name: str) -> str:
    """Get a personalized greeting"""
    return f"Hello, {name}!"

@mcp.prompt()
def review_code(code: str) -> str:
    return f"Please review this code:\n\n{code}"
```

The preceding code does the following:

- Creates an MCP server instance with the name Demo
- Adds a tool called `multiply` that takes two numbers as input and returns their sum
- Adds a resource called `greeting` that takes a name as input and returns a personalized greeting
- Creates a prompt called `review_code` that takes a code snippet as input and returns a review of the code

Step 4: Test the server with the inspector

Here, we will use the inspector to test the server. The inspector is a CLI tool that can present both a UI and a CLI interface. The latter is meant for scripting and automation. The UI is meant for manual testing and debugging:

1. Run the following command in the terminal:

   ```
   mcp dev server.py
   ```

   This will start the inspector tool on port 6274.

2. Navigate to http://localhost:6274 in your web browser. This should start a web server with a visual interface, allowing you to test the sample.

3. In the visual interface, ensure you fill in the fields like so:

   - **Command:** "mcp"
   - **Arguments:** "run server.py"

   Click **Connect**.

4. Select the **Tools** tab and **List Tools**, and **multiply** should be listed. Click **multiply** and fill in the fields like so:

   - **first:** 2
   - **second:** 4

   You should see the result **8** in the **Tool Result** field.

Great, now we have a working server, and we can test it using the inspector.

Step 5: Test the server with the inspector in CLI mode

In this subsection, we will run the inspector directly in CLI mode. The inspector is a Node.js app, and mcp dev is a wrapper around it.

At the time of this writing, mcp dev does not support all the features made available in the inspector. We will therefore show how to run the inspector directly as a Node.js app as that's what it's been written in.

Let's show some useful commands you can run in the inspector:

- **List tools:** Run the following command in the terminal:

```
npx @modelcontextprotocol/inspector --cli mcp run server.py --method
tools/list
```

This will list all the tools available on the server, and you should see the following output:

```
{
  "tools": [
    {
      "name": "multiply",
      "description": "Multiply two numbers",
      "inputSchema": {
        "type": "object",
```

```
      "properties": {
        "first": {
          "title": "First",
          "type": "integer"
        },
        "second": {
          "title": "Second",
          "type": "integer"
        }
      },
      "required": [
        "first",
        "second"
      ],
      "title": "multiplyArguments"
    },
    "outputSchema": {
      "type": "object",
      "properties": {
        "result": {
          "title": "Result",
          "type": "integer"
        }
      },
      "required": [
        "result"
      ],
      "title": "multiplyOutput"
    }
  }
 ]
}
```

Here, you see all the tools on the server in JSON format. We only have one tool, `multiply`, but we can see that it has an `inputSchema` with `first` and `second` parameters.

- **Call a tool**: Run the following command in the terminal:

```
npx @modelcontextprotocol/inspector --cli mcp run server.py --method
tools/call --tool-name multiply --tool-arg first=2 --tool-arg
second=4
```

You should see a response like this:

```
{
  "content": [
    {
      "type": "text",
      "text": "8"
    }
  ],
  "structuredContent": {
    "result": "8"
  },
  "isError": false
}
```

- **List resources**: Run the following command in the terminal:

```
npx @modelcontextprotocol/inspector --cli mcp run server.py --method
resources/list
```

This will list all the resources available in the server, and you should see the following output:

```
{
  "resources": []
}
```

Empty? The reason is that there's a difference between a resource and a templated resource. Here's how you can list the templated resources:

```
npx @modelcontextprotocol/inspector --cli mcp run server.py --method
resources/templates/list
```

You should get a response like this:

```
{
  "resourceTemplates": [
```

```
    {
      "uriTemplate": "greeting://{name}",
      "name": "get_greeting",
      "description": "Get a personalized greeting"
    }
  ]
}
```

- Let's call our templated resource:

```
npx @modelcontextprotocol/inspector --cli mcp run server.py --method
resources/read --uri greeting://chris
```

You should see a response like this:

```
{
  "contents": [
    {
      "uri": "greeting://chris",
      "mimeType": "text/plain",
      "text": "Hello, chris!"
    }
  ]
}
```

- Let's list prompts next with the following command:

```
npx @modelcontextprotocol/inspector --cli mcp run server.py --method
prompts/list
```

You should see an output similar to the following:

```
{
  "prompts": [
    {
      "name": "review_code",
      "description": "",
      "arguments": [
        {
          "name": "code",
          "required": true
```

```
            }
        ]
    }
]
}
```

- To call a prompt, we would type the name of the prompt and `prompts/get`, like so:

```
npx @modelcontextprotocol/inspector --cli mcp run server.py
--method prompts/get --prompt-name review_code --prompt-args
code="print('Hello World')"
```

You should see a response like this:

```
{
  "messages": [
    {
      "role": "user",
      "content": {
        "type": "text",
        "text": "Please review this code:\n\nprint('Hello World')"
      }
    }
  ]
}
```

Optionally, you could add a resource in `server.py`, like so:

```
@mcp.resource("command://ping")
def get_echo() -> str:
    """Send pong"""
    return "Pong"
```

Read it like so:

```
npx @modelcontextprotocol/inspector --cli mcp run server.py --method
resources/read --uri command://ping
```

You should see a response like this:

```
{
  "contents": [
    {
```

```
        "uri": "command://ping",
        "mimeType": "text/plain",
        "text": "Pong"
      }
    ]
}
```

Note how you invoke resources and resource templates in the same way using the `uri` parameter.

Summary

In this chapter, we covered how to build your first server. For our first server, we used the STDIO transport to create a server meant to be run on our machine. We also looked into various ways of testing out the server features using a tool called the inspector. The inspector tool has two different modalities, CLI mode and visual mode. The former mode is used for CI/CD scenarios, and the latter for you as a developer quickly trying out features.

In our upcoming chapter, we'll describe the SSE transport, which you can use if you want the server to be consumed via a URL address.

Assignment — an e-commerce STDIO server

For this MCP server, we will add capabilities that can be used in the context of an e-commerce application. Therefore, the server will need the following features.

It will need these tools:

- `get-orders`: This tool will return a list of orders. The optional input is a customer ID, and the output is a list of orders. Each order should contain the following fields: ID, customer ID, quantity, total price, and status.
- `get-order`: This tool will return a specific order. The input is the order ID, and the output is an order. The order should contain the following fields: ID, customer ID, quantity, total price, and status.
- `place-order`: This tool will place an order. The input is the customer ID and the cart ID.
- `get-cart`: This tool will return a cart.
- `get-cart-items`: This tool will return a list of items in the cart. The input is the cart ID, and the output is a list of items. Each item should contain the following fields: ID, name, description, price, quantity, and product ID.

- add-to-cart: This tool will add an item to the cart. The input is the cart ID, product ID, and quantity. The output is a success message. If the cart ID is not provided, the tool should create a new cart and add the item to the new cart. The output should be a success message and the cart ID.

- products: This tool will return a list of products. The optional input is a category, and the output is a list of products. The product should contain the following fields: ID, name, description, price, and category. The output should be in JSON format.

- product: This tool should return a specific product. The input is the product ID, and the output is a product. The product should contain the following fields: name, description, price, category, and ID. The output should be in JSON format.

- categories: This tool will return a list of categories. The output should be in JSON format. The categories should contain the following fields: ID, name, and description. The output should be in JSON format.

- get-customers: This tool will return a list of customers. The output should be in JSON format. It should contain the following fields: ID, name, and email.

It will need this resource:

- product_catalog: This resource will return a list of products in the catalog. The optional input is a category, and the output is a list of products. Each product should contain the following fields: name, description, and category. The idea is that the resource will return a list of products in the catalog, in case potential customers want to see them.

As you can see, this will support a simple e-commerce application and a customer trying to either put items in a cart or place an order.

You can keep state within memory data structures.

Solution

You can find the solution at https://github.com/PacktPublishing/Learn-Model-Context-Protocol-with-Python/blob/main/Chapter03/solutions/README.md.

Quiz

What of the following is something a server can expose?

- A: Tools, prompts, and services

- B: Tools and prompts

- C: Prompts, tools, and resources

You can find the solution at `https://github.com/PacktPublishing/Learn-Model-Context-Protocol-with-Python/blob/main/Chapter03/solutions/solution-quiz.md`.

References

- **Inspector tool**: `https://github.com/modelcontextprotocol/inspector`
- **Model Context Protocol**: `https://github.com/modelcontextprotocol/`
- **Python SDK**: `https://github.com/modelcontextprotocol/python-sdk`

4

Building SSE Servers

So far, you've seen how you can build MCP servers using STDIO as transport. That's a great choice of transport for servers meant to run locally. However, if you want to connect to servers remotely via HTTP or if you want responses from LLMs streamed, then there's another transport called **Server-Sent Events (SSE)** better suited to this scenario.

In this chapter, we'll focus on building and testing MCP servers using SSE as transport.

The chapter covers the following topics:

- SSE concepts
- Creating an SSE server as a web app
- Testing with SSE
- Creating an SSE server

Let's dive into the details of SSE and how to build a server using it.

SSE concepts

There are some concepts we need to understand before we can start building our server. First off, a server using SSE as transport is a server that can be accessed via HTTP. That means, even if it can run locally, it can also be accessed remotely. The implications of this are that this is a server that we need to expose using a web server.

SSE is a standard for unidirectional communication from server to client over a single, long-lived HTTP connection. It allows servers to push real-time updates to clients without requiring the client to poll for changes. Here are some more details:

- **Protocol**: SSE uses standard HTTP with the MIME type text/event-stream
- **Client API**: The browser uses the EventSource API to receive events
- **Format**: Messages are sent as plain text with fields such as event, data, and id, each terminated by two endlines

It's typically used for dashboard-like applications where real-time updates are crucial.

In MCP, SSE is split up into two parts: the part where we connect to the server and perform initialization (e.g., *handshake*), and a message part where we apply messages to the server that ends up reading or writing data. So, we need to implement the following endpoints:

- **SSE endpoint**: This endpoint is used as a way to handshake the connection between the client and the server. By sending a request to this endpoint, the client will receive a response that will keep the connection open.
- **Message endpoint**: This endpoint is what's used to route messages to the MCP server and its features.

It should be said that, depending on the chosen runtime and SDK, you may need to implement these endpoints yourself, but for some runtimes, it happens under the hood. Regardless, it's good to know how it works and what the endpoints are doing.

Creating an SSE server as a web app

The big difference compared to using the STDIO transport is that we need to expose an SSE server as a web application. Depending on whether we use Python or TypeScript, that means we need to implement the necessary HTTP endpoints.

Specifically for Python, we need to leverage a framework supporting **Asynchronous Server Gateway Interface (ASGI)**. ASGI is a specification that allows Python web frameworks to handle asynchronous and synchronous code, making it ideal for modern web applications. Let us look at Starlette.

Starlette

Starlette is a lightweight ASGI framework that we will use to build our SSE server. Previously, we mentioned endpoints that needed to be implemented, and Starlette will help us with that. It provides a simple way to create an ASGI application and handle routing, middleware, and other features.

Let's look at how Starlette works and then explain in more detail how to build an SSE server using it.

A typical application using Starlette will look like this:

```python
from starlette.applications import Starlette
from starlette.responses import JSONResponse
from starlette.routing import Route


async def homepage(request):
    return JSONResponse({'hello': 'world'})


app = Starlette(debug=True, routes=[
    Route('/', homepage),
])
```

In the preceding code, we've done the following:

- Imported the necessary modules from Starlette
- Defined a simple homepage function that returns a JSON response

The next step is to run it. We can use a server such as `uvicorn` to run our Starlette application:

```
uvicorn main:app
```

Here, we are using `uvicorn` to run the application. The syntax is `uvicorn <filename>:<name of app instance>`. In this case, the filename is `main.py` and the app instance is app.

Starlette and MCP

To use Starlette with MCP, we can create the following application:

```python
from starlette.applications import Starlette
from starlette.routing import Mount, Host
from mcp.server.fastmcp import FastMCP


mcp = FastMCP("My App")

# Mount the SSE server to the existing ASGI server
app = Starlette(
    routes=[
        Mount('/', app=mcp.sse_app()),
    ]
)

# or dynamically mount as host
app.router.routes.append(Host('mcp.acme.corp', app=mcp.sse_app()))
```

In the preceding code, we are doing the following:

- Importing the necessary modules from Starlette and MCP.
- Creating an instance of FastMCP with the name of the application. Note especially the mcp. sse_app() method. This is the method that creates the SSE server and mounts it to the existing ASGI server. What happens under the hood is that it creates the SSE endpoint and the message endpoint for you.

If you're interested in diving into the Python SDK to see how this is done, you can check https://github.com/modelcontextprotocol/python-sdk/blob/e80c0 150e1c2e45f66195d3cf7d209be31ce6e5d/src/mcp/server/fastmcp/server. py#L747, and you will see the following code as part of the sse_app() method:

```
routes.append(
    Route(
        self.settings.sse_path,
        endpoint=sse_endpoint,
        methods=["GET"],
    )
)
routes.append(
    Mount(
        self.settings.message_path,
        app=sse.handle_post_message,
    )
)
```

As you can see, both the SSE endpoint and the message endpoint are created for you by calling the sse_app() method.

What about features using SSE, do they work the same way as STDIO? Yes, they do. You can use the same decorators and methods to create features. The only difference is that you need to use the mcp.sse_app() method to create the SSE server and mount it to the existing ASGI server.

Testing with SSE

There are differences, though, when it comes to how testing tools using SSE work. Let's list the differences:

- **Inspector tool**: The **Inspector** tool is a command-line tool that allows you to test your server using both a visual interface and a command-line interface. The difference between STDIO and SSE is that you need to specify **Transport Type** as **SSE** and **URL** as http://<address>:<port>/sse. This is something you need to do when using the visual interface.

For the CLI mode, you need to specify a URL instead of how to run the server. So, the following command will work, provided you have the server running at localhost:8000:

```
npx @modelcontextprotocol/inspector --cli http:localhost:8000/sse
--method tools/list
```

Let's see the difference in the visual interface:

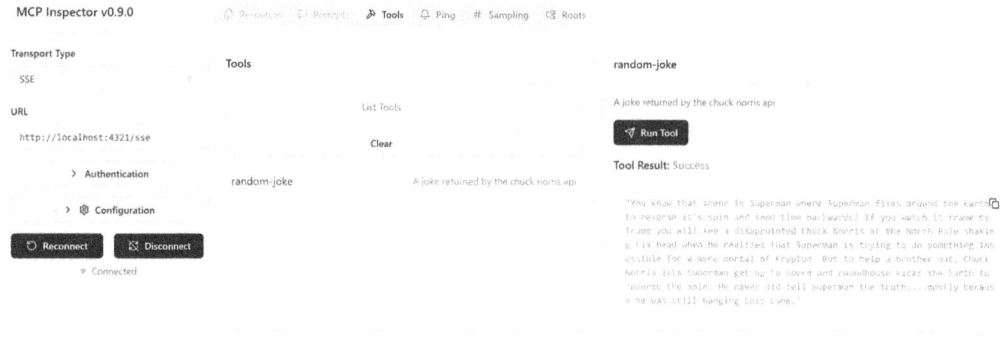

Figure 4.1 – Inspector tool, visual mode, SSE

🔍**Quick tip**: Need to see a high-resolution version of this image? Open this book in the next-gen Packt Reader or view it in the PDF/ePub copy.

📖**The next-gen Packt Reader** and a **free PDF/ePub copy** of this book are included with your purchase. Scan the QR code OR visit https://packtpub.com/unlock, then use the search bar to find this book by name. Double-check the edition shown to make sure you get the right one.

Note how **Transport Type** is set to SSE and **URL** is set to http://localhost:8000/sse. Remember with STDIO how we didn't have a **URL** field and rather a field to specify how to run the server? This is the difference between STDIO and SSE when it comes to the Inspector tool.

- **Web client**: Because the SSE server is running on HTTP, you can use any HTTP client to test it. This includes tools such as Postman, cURL, or even your web browser. To use cURL, you can use the following command:

  1. Get the session ID:

```
export MCP_SERVER="http://0.0.0.0:8000"
curl "${MCP_SERVER}/sse"
```

This will produce a response like this:

```
```text
event: endpoint
data: http://localhost:5001/messages?session_id=<my session
id>
```
```

  2. Use the session ID to send a message to the server on the message endpoint.

> Ensure you send this in another terminal instance. The answer to this request will appear in the first terminal though.

```
export MCP_ENDPOINT="http://localhost:8000/messages?session_
id=<my session id>"
```

  3. Send a message to the server, such as listing tools, in a separate terminal from the one that you sent the initialize request to.

```
curl -X POST "${MCP_ENDPOINT}" -H "Content-Type: application/
json" -d '{
  "jsonrpc": "2.0",
  "id": 1,
  "method": "tools/list"
}'
```

So, yes, it's possible to do this using cURL, but it's a bit cumbersome, which makes the inspector tool a great choice for testing your server – also for SSE.

Creating an SSE server

Okay, so we understand the concepts of SSE and how to build a server, and even how our testing tools work and are different from STDIO. Now it's time to build our own SSE server. We'll learn how to do the following:

1. Set up a project

2. Add the server code

3. Test the server

Create the project

Let's create a new project like so:

1. Create a virtual environment:

    ```
    python -m venv venv
    ```

2. Activate the virtual environment:

    ```
    source venv/bin/activate
    ```

3. Install the dependencies:

    ```
    pip install "mcp[cli]"
    ```

There, you should be all set up to start building your SSE server.

Add the server code

Now add the following code to your project:

In server.py, add the following code:

```
from starlette.applications import Starlette
from starlette.routing import Mount, Host
from mcp.server.fastmcp import FastMCP


mcp = FastMCP("My App")

# Mount the SSE server to the existing ASGI server
app = Starlette(
    routes=[
```

```
            Mount('/', app=mcp.sse_app()),
    ]
)
```

In the preceding code, we've done the following:

- Imported the necessary modules from Starlette and MCP.

- Created an instance of `FastMCP` with the name of the application. Note especially the `mcp.sse_app()` method helping us mount the endpoints for SSE handshake and message routing.

Add features

The next step is about adding features to your server. As mentioned, there's no difference between STDIO and SSE when it comes to features. You can use the same decorators and methods to create features.

In the same file, add the following code:

```
@mcp.tool()
def add(a: int, b: int) -> int:
    """calc"""
    return a + b
```

You'll get the chance to add more features later in the assignment, but for now, you have a working server with a feature that adds two numbers.

Run it

The next step is to run the server.

1. Start the server using the command line:

```
uvicorn main:app --port 3000
```

> The syntax is uvicorn `<filename>`:`<app>`, where `<filename>` is the name of your Python file and `<app>` is the name of your ASGI app.

2. Start the **Inspect** tool using the command line:

```
mcp dev server.py
```

Set the following fields in the UI:

- **Transport Type: SSE**
- **URL:** `http://localhost:3000/sse`

Try your features as usual, but now using the SSE server.

Test it

We will test our server in three different ways.

- **Inspector tool, as a visual interface**: This is a good way to test your server and see how it works
- **Inspector tool with the CLI option**: The CLI option provides a response directly in the command line. This is a good way to test your servers in, for example, CI/CD pipelines.
- **Using a client**: Here, we'll use cURL to test that our server responds to requests. This is a good way to quickly test your server.

Inspector tool

Let's try the Inspector tool using the visual interface. Start the Inspector tool using the command line:

> Run the following command in a new terminal window with the server running.

```
npx @modelcontextprotocol/inspector
```

Set the following fields in the UI:

- **Transport Type: SSE**
- **URL:** `http://localhost:3000/sse`

In the **Tools** section, select **add** and type the input for **a** and **b**:

```
5
10
```

Inspector tool as a CLI option

For this option, we'll use the Inspector tool like before, but with the added --cli option to run it in CLI mode. Remember, we will get the response directly in the command line as opposed to the UI:

```
npx @modelcontextprotocol/inspector --cli http://127.0.0.1:3000/sse
--method tools/call --tool-name add --tool-arg a=5 --tool-arg b=10
```

You should see the following output:

```
{
  "content": [
    {
      "type": "text",
      "text": "15"
    }
  ],
  "structuredContent": {
    "result": 15
  },
  "isError": false
}
```

curl command

To test with cURL, there are three calls we need to make:

1. A call to /sse. This should give us a session ID back:

   ```
   curl http://127.0.0.1:3000/sse
   ```

   You should see an output similar to the following:

   ```
   event: endpoint
   data: /messages/?session_id=53ddee76d5ec4b4aaa9420f24462210a
   ```

2. A call to /messages with the session ID also containing the initialized MCP message.

   > The following command should be run in a *separate terminal*.

```
curl -X POST "http://127.0.0.1:3000/messages/?session_
id=53ddee76d5ec4b4aaa9420f24462210a" -H "Content-Type: application/
json" -d '{
    "jsonrpc": "2.0",
    "method": "notifications/initialized"
}'
```

This will tell the server we're ready to communicate.

3. **Feature ask:** the following `curl` command is asking to list tools on the MCP Server.

> The following command should be run in the *same terminal as the previous command.*

```
curl -X POST "http://127.0.0.1:3000/
messages/?sessionId=53ddee76d5ec4b4aaa9420f24462210a" -H "Content-
Type: application/json" -d '{
    "jsonrpc": "2.0",
    "id": 1,
    "method": "tools/list",
    "params": {}
}'
```

You should now see a response in the *first terminal* you used when you initialized the connection. It should look similar to the following:

```
event:message
data: {"result":{"tools":[{"name":"products","description":"get
products by category","inputSchema":{"type":"object","properties":
{"category":{"type":"string"}},"additionalProperties":false,"$schema":
"http://json-schema.org/draft-07/schema#"}},{"name":"cart-list",
"description":"get products in cart","inputSchema":{"type":"object",
"properties":{},"additionalProperties":false,"$schema":"http://json-
schema.org/draft-07/schema#"}},{"name":"cart-
add","description":"Adding
products to
cart","inputSchema":{"type":"object","properties":{"title":
{"type":"string"}},"additionalProperties":false,"$schema":
"http://json-schema.org/draft-07/
```

```
schema#"}},{"name":"add","inputSchema"
:{"type":"object","properties":{"a":{"type":"number"},"b":{"type":
"number"}},"required":["a","b"],"additionalProperties":false,"$schema"
:"http://json-schema.org/draft-07/
schema#"}}]},"jsonrpc":"2.0","id":1}
```

As a recommendation, I prefer to use the Inspector tool as it provides a better experience and is easier to use. The `curl` command is more of a low-level approach and could be nice to use to get an initial session ID. It does tell you how the underlying protocol works, which can be helpful for debugging.

Summary

In this chapter, we learned about SSE and how to build a server using it.

We also learned about the differences between STDIO and SSE when it comes to testing tools and how to use the Inspector tool with SSE. The difference is that STDIO listens to `stdin` and `stdout` while SSE listens to HTTP requests. SSE can also be used to stream responses from LLMs.

Finally, we built our own SSE server and tested it using the Inspector tool and cURL.

In the next chapter, we will look into another transport called Streamable HTTP, which is the preferred transport to use when exposing a server via a URL.

Assignment — SSE server

In this assignment, you will build out an SSE server with some features to support the following use cases:

- List products by category
- Add products to cart
- List products in cart

You can use the code provided in this chapter as a starting point.

Solution

You can access the solution at https://github.com/PacktPublishing/Learn-Model-Context-Protocol-with-Python/blob/main/Chapter04/solutions/README.md.

Quiz

What is the SSE transport used for?

- A: To expose a server via HTTP
- B: To expose a server via STDIO
- C: To enable streaming of responses from LLMs

Which routes are used for SSE?

- A: `/mcp`
- B: `/sse`
- C: `/messages`

You can access the solution at `https://github.com/PacktPublishing/Learn-Model-Context-Protocol-with-Python/blob/main/Chapter04/solutions/solution-quiz.md`.

References

- Lifecycle: `https://modelcontextprotocol.info/specification/draft/basic/lifecycle/`
- Starlette: `https://www.starlette.io/`
- Transports: `https://modelcontextprotocol.io/docs/concepts/transports`

Unlock this book's exclusive benefits now   **UNLOCK NOW**

Scan this QR code or go to `https://packtpub.com/unlock`, then search this book by name.

Note: Keep your purchase invoice ready before you start.

5

Streamable HTTP

In *Chapter 4*, we discussed building MCP servers with the **Server-Sent Events (SSE)** transport. In that chapter, you learned that if you want users to access your MCP server on the web, you can't use STDIO, but instead you need to use a transport such as SSE or, as described in this chapter, Streamable HTTP.

So, in this chapter, you will learn about the following:

- The Streamable HTTP transport
- Why this transport should be used over SSE
- How to work with concepts such as notifications and resumability

The chapter covers the following topics:

- Streamable HTTP versus SSE, and why it is the new standard
- Streamable HTTP in MCP
- Resumability
- Notifications
- Creating and testing a server with Streamable HTTP
- Testing the server
- Testing resumability

Streamable HTTP versus SSE, and why it is the new standard

The differences between SSE and Streamable HTTP are important to understand when choosing the right technology for your application.

There are some key distinctions. The first reason is that SSE in MCP is considered **deprecated**; you should be using Streamable HTTP instead.

So, why is there a chapter called *SSE* in this book? The reason is that this book is written for you as both a developer of MCP servers and also as a consumer of servers, where you might be writing a client toward an existing server that might be using SSE. In short, you should know how to deal with both types of transport due to there being legacy code that you might be asked to work with. In fact, the article at `https://github.com/modelcontextprotocol/modelcontextprotocol/discussions/308` states that 20 reference servers, over 50 official integrations, and 186 community-developed servers and clients were using SSE when it was announced that it was deprecated. This means when you develop for MCP, ensure you keep in mind that you need to handle both SSE and Streamable HTTP, even if you develop new servers in Streamable HTTP.

Okay, but why the deprecation decision? Well, there are several reasons why Streamable HTTP is a better choice:

- **Single endpoint simplicity**: Clients and servers communicate via a single endpoint (e.g., `/mcp`), supporting both `POST` and `GET` methods. This simplifies implementation and reduces connection overhead.

- **Resumability support**: Streamable HTTP supports resumable sessions using headers such as `Last-Event-ID` and `Mcp-Session-ID`, allowing clients to reconnect and resume streams reliably. This is a powerful feature where, when clients lose connection, they can resume connection and start receiving data from where they were before the disconnect rather than starting from the beginning.

- **Better compatibility**: It works seamlessly with modern HTTP infrastructure—load balancers, proxies, and API gateways—where SSE often fails or requires workarounds.

- **Bidirectional communication**: While SSE is unidirectional, Streamable HTTP can be upgraded to support bidirectional flows, making it more versatile for agent-to-agent or client-server interactions.

- **Future-proofing**: Streamable HTTP aligns with evolving MCP standards and community best practices. It's modular, extensible, and designed for stateless or session-based models. Stateless servers are more lightweight and easier to construct, and being able to choose the right model for the right scenario is a compelling argument.

Streamable HTTP in MCP

Okay, so normally when we're talking about streaming, some of you might think of how you divide up files in chunks or how you have AI models return their response in smaller parts. However, in the context of MCP, streaming is more about how we transmit data over HTTP while following the *streamable* standard, meaning that clients using Streamable HTTP typically send the following Accept header: `Accept: application/json, text/event-stream`.

This tells the server the client can handle both batch JSON responses and streamed events (via SSE). The server can choose the appropriate response mode based on the request type and context.

Is that it, streaming that just sends simple responses? There's a bit more to it, namely, resumability.

Resumability

Resumability is a concept that means that, if a client loses connection with a server while data is being transferred, upon reconnecting with the server, it can resume the data exchange where it was, rather than starting from the beginning. For long-running operations, this can be a game-changer. Technically, resumability can be achieved by both SSE and Streamable HTTP, but within the context of the MCP protocol, it's only supported for Streamable HTTP.

Let's illustrate it with a diagram:

Figure 5.1 – Resumability

As you can see from the preceding diagram, the client doesn't have to restart from the beginning but can resume where they were. This works because the client, upon reconnecting, sends mcp-session-id and last-event-id headers. It's important to note that upon disconnecting, the client needs to do so gracefully, so it stores these two headers for later use.

What needs to be done on the server side to support this, though? Well, the server needs to do the following for resumability to work:

1.   Create a session store, which is where produced messages are placed.

2.   Set up a middleware that handles incoming requests and outgoing responses to ensure messages are properly stored and can be retrieved for resuming sessions. Exactly how this happens differs between frameworks:

```python
# 1. Creates an in-memory store, you should use a persistent store
in a production scenario
event_store = InMemoryEventStore()


# 2. Create the session manager with our app and event store
session_manager = StreamableHTTPSessionManager(
    app=app,
    event_store=event_store,  # Enable resumability
    json_response=json_response,
)


# 3. Starts a session manager
@contextlib.asynccontextmanager
    async def lifespan(app: Starlette) -> AsyncIterator[None]:
        """Context manager for managing session
            manager lifecycle."""
        async with session_manager.run():
            logger.info("Application started with
                StreamableHTTP session manager!")
            try:
                yield
            finally:
                logger.info("Application shutting down…")


# 4. Creating the web server and assigning a lifespan handler
starlette_app = Starlette(
    debug=True,
    routes=[
        Mount("/mcp", app=handle_streamable_http),
    ],
    lifespan=lifespan,
)
```

💡 **Quick tip**: Enhance your coding experience with the **AI Code Explainer** and **Quick Copy** features. Open this book in the next-gen Packt Reader. Click the **Copy** button

(1) to quickly copy code into your coding environment, or click the **Explain** button

(2) to get the AI assistant to explain a block of code to you.

```
                                                              Copy        Explain
function calculate(a, b) {                                     1            2
  return {sum: a + b};
};
```

📕 **The next-gen Packt Reader** is included for free with the purchase of this book. Scan the QR code OR go to `https://packtpub.com/unlock`, then use the search bar to find this book by name. Double-check the edition shown to make sure you get the right one.

Let's break down this code:

- We start by creating a session store that will help store and retrieve messages.
- Then, we create a session manager that controls the access to the store of the `StreamableHTTPSessionManager` type.
- We start the session manager and create the web server with the appropriate lifespan handler.
- Finally, we create the web server and assign the lifespan handler.

There, everything is set up, and any client can now connect to the server and start a session.

Okay, now that we understand a bit more about how resumability can really improve the user experience, as the client can get messages where they were when the disconnect happened, let's talk about another concept, namely, notifications.

Notifications

Notifications are not a concept unique to Streamable HTTP but can also be used in SSE. However, paired with resumability, they suddenly become very powerful. Let's describe what they are first and then discuss how they relate to resumability.

Notifications come in many different forms to communicate that something important has happened. They are real-time updates and, for the sake of the SDK, are handled as a separate thing. That means the SDK provides a special way to listen to notifications by implementing a handler for them, as you will soon see.

Here are some scenarios where notifications make sense:

- Status updates
- Progress notifications
- Error messages
- Informational messages

For example, the final message sent from the client to the server is a notification called `notifications/initialized` and signals that the client and the server can exchange non-handshake messages and more normal operations such as listing tools, reading a resource, and so on. The following is the JSON-RPC shape of the `notifications/initialized` message:

```
{
  "jsonrpc": "2.0",
  "method": "notifications/initialized"
}
```

Producing a notification

How do we produce a notification? Well, a notification is nothing more than a JSON-RPC message, and your SDK usually has a dedicated method to make it easier to send notifications. As there are different types of notifications, it's more a matter of using the right method with the appropriate parameters.

To produce a notification, we need a reference to the context object, which we can add as an input parameter in our tool, for example. Once we have that reference, we can call specific notification methods such as debug, info, warning, and error. Each method has its own purpose, such as sending debug info, informational messages, warning messages, and error messages:

```
from mcp.server.session import ServerSession


# 1. Get a hold of the context object
@mcp.tool(description="A simple tool returning file content")
async def echo(message: str,
    ctx: ctx: Context[ServerSession, None]) -> str:


    # 2. Select the appropriate method for sending the correct
    notification type
    await ctx.debug(f"Debug: Processing '{data}'")
    await ctx.info("Info: Starting processing")
    await ctx.warning("Warning: This is experimental")
    await ctx.error("Error: (This is just a demo)")


    return "Final result"
```

In this code, the echo tool will produce four different notifications and a final result.

Handling a notification

When you consume notifications as a client, they show up in a different place than where you would normally expect them. Instead of being part of the regular message flow, they are handled separately with their own callbacks:

```
# 1. Define the message handler

def message_handler(
    message: RequestResponder[types.ServerRequest, types.ClientResult]
    | types.ServerNotification
    | Exception,) -> None:
    print("Received message:", message)
    if isinstance(message, Exception):
        raise message
    else:
```

```
        if isinstance(message, types.ServerNotification):
            print("NOTIFICATION:", message)
        elif isinstance(message, RequestResponder):
            print("REQUEST_RESPONDER:", message)
        else:
            print("SERVER_REQUEST:", message)


# 2. Create the client session and assign message handler to message_
handler property
async with ClientSession(
    read_stream,
    write_stream,

    message_handler=message_handler,
) as session:

    await session.initialize()

    print("Session initialized, ready to call tools.")

    # Call a tool
    tool_result = await session.call_tool("echo", {"message": "hello"})
```

In this client, we do the following:

1. Define the message handler; the handler is capable of taking different types of messages and processing them accordingly.

2. Create the client session and assign a message handler to the message_handler property.

We also observe that normal feature responses, such as calling a tool or reading a resource, are handled the normal way, whereas notifications are dealt with via the message handler, message_handler.

Notifications in the Inspector tool

Great, now that we have a sense for how to set up sending notifications and receiving them, let's see how notifications appear in our Inspector tool, as we need to learn to look for them in the right place.

If you start the Inspector tool in a visual mode, you will see a screen like this:

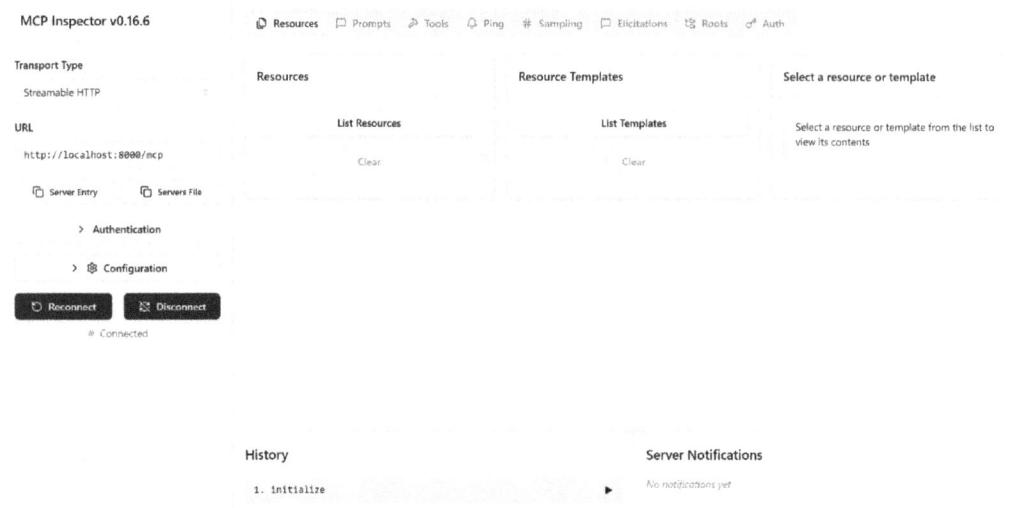

| MCP Inspector v0.16.6 | ⚙ Resources ⬜ Prompts ⬿ Tools ⬀ Ping # Sampling ⬜ Elicitations ↹ Roots ♂ Auth |

Transport Type
Streamable HTTP

URL
http://localhost:8000/mcp

⬚ Server Entry   ⬚ Servers File

> Authentication

> ⚙ Configuration

[↻ Reconnect] [✕ Disconnect]

● Connected

Resources

List Resources

Clear

Resource Templates

List Templates

Clear

Select a resource or template

Select a resource or template from the list to view its contents

History

1. initialize   ▶

Server Notifications

No notifications yet

Figure 5.2 – Inspector tool

> 🔍 **Quick tip**: Need to see a high-resolution version of this image? Open this book in the next-gen Packt Reader or view it in the PDF/ePub copy.
>
> 📖 **The next-gen Packt Reader** and a **free PDF/ePub copy** of this book are included with your purchase. Scan the QR code OR visit `https://packtpub.com/unlock`, then use the search bar to find this book by name. Double-check the edition shown to make sure you get the right one.

Now, if you run a tool, you will see the tool result, and you will see an area below it showing notifications, like so:

🖅 Run Tool

Tool Result: Success

Structured Content:

```
{
    result: "Here's the file content: hello"
}
```

✓ Valid according to output schema

Unstructured Content:

⚠ No text block matches structured content

```
"Here's the file content: hello"
```

Server Notifications

3. notifications/message ▼

Details:

```
{
    method: "notifications/message"
    params: {
        level: "info"
        data: "Processing file 3/3:"
```

Figure 5.3 – Notifications

Notifications with resumability

As we said before, notifications can be sent with SSE and Streamable HTTP, but with the latter, it becomes extra important. Imagine you have a client that disconnects a number of times due to a spotty internet connection, but thanks to logic in the client performing reconnects and resumability support in the server, the end user still has a good experience, as they won't miss out on either notifications or normal messages, such as a tool response, for example.

Now, let's move on to creating a server.

Creating and testing a server with Streamable HTTP

Let's create a server, and in doing so, we'll also integrate notifications. After the server is built, in the next section, we'll try testing it out with the different tools we have at our disposal, such as writing our own client, using the Inspector tool, and testing with cURL.

To create the server code, there are a few things we need to do:

1. Set up the transport as Streamable HTTP.
2. Add features.
3. Add code that sends notifications when a tool is called.

Great, now that we have our plan in place, let's implement it. Here's an attempt to implement the first two points of our plan:

```python
# server.py
from mcp.server.fastmcp import FastMCP, Context
from typing import Optional, Dict, Any, List, AsyncGenerator
from mcp.types import (
    LoggingMessageNotificationParams,
    TextContent
)

# Create an MCP server
mcp = FastMCP("Streamable DEMO")

# 2. Adding features
@mcp.tool(description="A simple tool returning file content")
async def echo(message: str, ctx: Context) -> str:
```

```
    return f"Here's the file content: {message}"
```

```
# 1. Set up the transport as streamable HTTP.
mcp.run(transport="streamable-http")
```

To add sending notifications, we need to add the Context object to our method signature, like so:

```
@mcp.tool(description="A simple tool returning file content")
async def echo(message: str, ctx: Context) -> str:
```

Let's finally add the part in the tool where it produces a notification using the Context object:

```
@mcp.tool(description="A simple tool returning file content")
async def echo(message: str, ctx: Context) -> str:

    # 3. Send a notification
    await ctx.info(f"Processing file 1/3:")
    await ctx.info(f"Processing file 2/3:")
    await ctx.info(f"Processing file 3/3:")

    return f"Here's the file content: {message}"
```

Our full code now looks like this:

```
from mcp.server.fastmcp import FastMCP, Context
from typing import Optional, Dict, Any, List, AsyncGenerator
from mcp.types import (
    LoggingMessageNotificationParams,
    TextContent
)

# Create an MCP server
mcp = FastMCP("Streamable DEMO")

# 2. Adding features
@mcp.tool(description="A simple tool returning file content")
async def echo(message: str, ctx: Context) -> str:
    # 3. Send a notification
    await ctx.info(f"Processing file 1/3:")
    await ctx.info(f"Processing file 2/3:")
```

```
    await ctx.info(f"Processing file 3/3:")

    return f"Here's the file content: {message}"

# 1. Set up the transport as streamable HTTP.
mcp.run(transport="streamable-http")
```

Let's look at testing our server next.

Testing the server

As always, we have different choices to try out the server functionality:

- Creating a client
- Using the Inspector tool
- Testing with cURL

Let's try out each of these options.

Using the Inspector tool

We covered the Inspector tool earlier in this chapter, but let's quickly remind ourselves how it works with our newly created server. We can call the Inspector tool like so to start up a web server. Select the following fields:

- **Transport Type: HTTP**
- **Server URL**: http://localhost:8000/mcp (adjust the port if necessary)

Click the **Connect** button to connect to the server so you can use its features and then enter the following:

```
npx @modelcontextprotocol/inspector
```

As you can see, it's very similar to testing SSE servers; just change the transport type and make sure your URL has /mcp at the end instead of /sse.

Testing with cURL

We introduced cURL in the previous chapter; we can use it here as well. To get a session ID, you will need to send an initialize message. The message should contain what capabilities you support, such as tools, for example.

Here's the message you need to send:

```
curl -X POST "http://127.0.0.1:8000/mcp" -H "Accept: text/event-stream,
application/json" -H "Content-Type: application/json" -d '{
  "jsonrpc": "2.0",
  "id": 1,
  "method": "initialize",
  "params": { "protocolVersion": "2025-03-26", "capabilities": { "tools":
{} }, "clientInfo": { "name": "ExampleClient", "version": "1.0.0" } }
}'
```

Note that you need to send `Accept` headers and content type. Make a note of the session ID returned, as you will use it for all remaining calls.

Create a second terminal window and then run the following command, but replace the `mcp-session-id` value with the session ID you got back in the previous step:

```
curl -X POST "http://127.0.0.1:8000/mcp" -H "Content-Type: application/
json" -H "Accept: text/event-stream, application/json" -H "mcp-session-id:
39a0b504364140ce97d8eded79b1c244" -d '{
    "jsonrpc": "2.0",
    "method": "notifications/initialized"
}'
```

Note how the session ID isn't a query parameter called `session_id` anymore, but a header value called `mcp-session-id`. The message you sent was a notification of the `notifications/initialized` type, meaning it's the last message of the handshake process. After this message, we can now do more normal things, such as listing tools, calling them, and so on, so let's do that next.

Replace the value for `mcp-session-id` and keep using the second terminal window, and then run the following command:

```
curl -X POST "http://127.0.0.1:8000/mcp" -H "Content-Type: application/
json" -H "Accept: text/event-stream, application/json" -H "mcp-session-id:
39a0b504364140ce97d8eded79b1c244" -d '{
    "jsonrpc": "2.0",
    "id": 1,
    "method": "tools/call",
    "params": {
```

```
        "name": "echo",
        "arguments": { "message": "chris" }
    }
}'
```

In this message of the tools/call type, we call a specific tool, echo, with the chris argument, and we should see a tool response similar to the following:

```
event: message
data: {"method":"notifications/
message","params":{"level":"info","data":"Processing file
1/3:"},"jsonrpc":"2.0"}


event: message
data: {"method":"notifications/
message","params":{"level":"info","data":"Processing file
2/3:"},"jsonrpc":"2.0"}


event: message
data: {"method":"notifications/
message","params":{"level":"info","data":"Processing file
3/3:"},"jsonrpc":"2.0"}


event: message
data:
{"jsonrpc":"2.0","id":1,"result":{"content":[{"type":"text","text":"Here's
the file content: chris"}],"structuredContent":{"result":"Here's the file
content: chris"},"isError":false}}
```

This response, in the second terminal window, says we got three notifications and a final tool response, which shows that our MCP server works as intended.

As you can see, both Inspector and cURL are good tools to use for testing out your server. Building a client, however, might be how we end up integrating our MCP server in a working solution, so let's look at that in our next section.

Creating a client to handle notifications

Let's talk about the client. Clients generally need to be instructed to also handle notifications. This is something that's seen as an extra thing needed in addition to the normal features. Let's work out an implementation plan next. Let's define our plan first:

1. Create a streamable HTTP transport and client.

2. Set up a notification handler.

3. Call a tool.

Addressing the first point in our plan, our code looks like so:

```python
# 1. Create a streamable HTTP transport and client
async with streamablehttp_client(f"http://localhost:{port}/mcp") as (
        read_stream,
        write_stream,
        session_callback,
    ):
        # Create a session using the client streams
        async with ClientSession(
            read_stream,
            write_stream
        ) as session:
```

Here, we use the `streamablehttp_client` function to create a Streamable HTTP client. Thereafter, we create a client instance by initiating `ClientSession`.

To support incoming notifications, we need to configure the client session by assigning it a function to a property called `message_handler`, like so:

```python
# 2. Set up a notification handler
async def message_handler(
        message: RequestResponder[types.ServerRequest, types.ClientResult]
        | types.ServerNotification
        | Exception,
    ) -> None:
        print("Received message:", message)
        if isinstance(message, Exception):
            raise message
        else:
            if isinstance(message, types.ServerNotification):
                print("NOTIFICATION:", message)
            elif isinstance(message, RequestResponder):
                print("REQUEST_RESPONDER:", message)
            else:
```

```
                        print("SERVER_REQUEST:", message)


    # omitted code for brevity


    async with ClientSession(
                read_stream,
                write_stream,
                message_handler=message_handler,
            ) as session:
```

Note how `message_handler` is assigned to `ClientSession` and how it points to a function called `message_handler`. The said function handles incoming messages and prints them out.

That's it, that's all we need to create a Streamable HTTP client and also support incoming notifications. Let's have a look at the full code:

```
from mcp.client.streamable_http import streamablehttp_client
from mcp import ClientSession
import asyncio
from typing import Optional, Dict, Any, List
import mcp.types as types

from mcp.types import (
    LoggingMessageNotificationParams,
    TextContent,
)

from mcp.shared.session import RequestResponder

port = 8000


# I get normal messages, notifications, and exceptions
# 2. Set up a notification handler
async def message_handler(
        message: RequestResponder[types.ServerRequest, types.ClientResult]
          | types.ServerNotification
          | Exception,
    ) -> None:
        print("Received message:", message)
```

```
            if isinstance(message, Exception):
                raise message

async def main():
    print("Starting client...")

    # 1. Create a streamable HTTP transport and client
    async with streamablehttp_client(f"http://localhost:{port}/mcp") as (
        read_stream,
        write_stream,
        session_callback,
    ):
        # 2. Set up a notification handler
        async with ClientSession(
            read_stream,
            write_stream,
            message_handler=message_handler,
        ) as session:

            # Initialize the connection
            await session.initialize()

            # 3. Call a tool
            results = []
            tool_result = await session.call_tool("echo",
                {"message": "hello"})

            print("Tool result:", tool_result)

asyncio.run(main())
```

Now, if we run the client, it will tell us that the notifications are indeed notifications:

```
NOTIFICATION: root=LoggingMessageNotification(method='notifications/
message', params=LoggingMessageNotificationParams(meta=None, level='info',
logger=None, data='Processing file 3/3:'), jsonrpc='2.0')
```

The conclusion is that by using the message_handler method, we can capture all messages, notifications, and exceptions that are sent from the server. This allows us to handle them appropriately and provide feedback to the user.

Testing out resumability

There's actually an example implementation in the SDK for resumability. Let's try that code out and see how it differs. You can find a simplified version of it at https://github.com/PacktPublishing/Learn-Model-Context-Protocol-with-Python/blob/main/Chapter05/solutions/resumability/README.md.

What the code does is define a server with one tool, process-files. Upon calling the tool, you get three notifications and one final response. The easiest way to test the server out is by using cURL. With cURL, we can perform the handshake process, call a tool, and even do the needed bespoke request so it replays events. Let's take it step by step:

1. Start the server first.

2. Start a second terminal and call curl with the following payload to exchange what features the client and the server both have:

```
curl -X POST "http://127.0.0.1:8000/mcp" -H "Accept: text/event-
stream, application/json" -H "Content-Type: application/json" -d '{
  "jsonrpc": "2.0",
  "id": 1,
  "method": "initialize",
  "params": { "protocolVersion": "2025-03-26", "capabilities":
{ "tools": {}, "logging": {} }, "clientInfo": { "name":
"ExampleClient", "version": "1.0.0" } }
}'
```

Check the terminal response in the first terminal window. You should see the server display session ID; copy that field for later use.

3. End the server-client handshake by sending an initialized notification; replace the mcp-session-id value with the value you just copied in the previous step:

```
curl -X POST "http://127.0.0.1:8000/mcp" -H "Content-Type:
application/json" -H "Accept: text/event-stream, application/json"
-H "mcp-session-id: 957f11af-4766-4c1c-a1f2-5bd6776cca6a" -d '{
    "jsonrpc": "2.0",
```

```
    "method": "notifications/initialized"
}'
```

4. Call the tool by pasting the following command in the second terminal window, making sure to replace the "mcp-session-id" value first:

```
curl -X POST "http://127.0.0.1:8000/mcp" -H "Content-Type:
application/json" -H "Accept: text/event-stream, application/json"
-H "mcp-session-id: 957f11af-4766-4c1c-a1f2-5bd6776cca6a" -d '{
    "jsonrpc": "2.0",
    "id": 1,
    "method": "tools/call",
    "params": {
      "name": "process-files",
      "arguments": { "message": "chris" }
    }
}'
```

At this point, you should see a bunch of notifications and the final result in the second terminal window, like so:

```
event: message
id: 3a9d76c3-36d8-45f3-bd6e-8b9c82826de8_1757284976937_z6m5xbyc
data: {"method":"notifications/
message","params":{"level":"info","data":"sales1.csv
processed"},"jsonrpc":"2.0"}

event: message
id: 3a9d76c3-36d8-45f3-bd6e-8b9c82826de8_1757284976940_meh2n52f
data: {"method":"notifications/
message","params":{"level":"info","data":"sales2.csv
processed"},"jsonrpc":"2.0"}

event: message
id: 3a9d76c3-36d8-45f3-bd6e-8b9c82826de8_1757284976943_e3v55tmn
data: {"method":"notifications/
message","params":{"level":"info","data":"sales3.csv
processed"},"jsonrpc":"2.0"}
```

```
event: message
id: 3a9d76c3-36d8-45f3-bd6e-8b9c82826de8_1757284976946_sgpvardt
data: {"result":{"content":[{"type":"text","text":"Files processed:
3"}]},"jsonrpc":"2.0","id":1}
```

Let's focus on the following message, a notification that says we're on file 2/3. Imagine we went into a tunnel and lost network connection. Make note of the ID, as this ID is the last you saw before losing connection:

```
event: message
id: 3a9d76c3-36d8-45f3-bd6e-8b9c82826de8_1757284976940_meh2n52f
data: {"method":"notifications/
message","params":{"level":"info","data":"sales2.csv
processed"},"jsonrpc":"2.0"}
```

5. In our final step, we need to send a GET request to the /mcp endpoint with the session ID and last event ID passed in the headers. That should lead to the server replaying all messages that we missed out on, which should be the sales3.csv file notification and the final tool result. Remember to replace both mcp-session-id and last-event-id before you paste the following in the second terminal window:

```
curl "http://127.0.0.1:8000/mcp" -H "Content-Type: application/json"
-H "Accept: text/event-stream, application/json" -H "mcp-session-id:
957f11af-4766-4c1c-a1f2-5bd6776cca6a" -H "last-event-id: 3a9d76c3-
36d8-45f3-bd6e-8b9c82826de8_1757284976940_meh2n52f"
```

Pasting this result means you should see the following in the second terminal window:

```
event: message
id: 3a9d76c3-36d8-45f3-bd6e-8b9c82826de8_1757284976943_e3v55tmn
data: {"method":"notifications/
message","params":{"level":"info","data":"sales3.csv
processed"},"jsonrpc":"2.0"}

event: message
id: 3a9d76c3-36d8-45f3-bd6e-8b9c82826de8_1757284976946_sgpvardt
data: {"result":{"content":[{"type":"text","text":"Files processed:
3"}]},"jsonrpc":"2.0","id":1}
```

Our one missing notification and the tool result! Isn't that great? We didn't lose any messages.

It should be said, though, that if you write code that can leverage replayability, you should listen to browser events when you lose network connection, so you have a chance to save the session ID and last event ID, and remember to call the server with GET /mcp rather than POST /mcp, as the latter would start a new session.

Also, if you use the event store I'm using, remember it's not good for production and that it would need to persist the message in a database or similar to be deemed production-ready.

Summary

In this chapter, we explored the concept of Streamable HTTP and how it differs from SSE. We learned that streaming allows for real-time data transmission, which is beneficial for applications that require immediate access to data, such as live events or large files.

Additionally, we implemented an MCP server that supports Streamable HTTP and demonstrated how to consume streaming data using the MCP SDK. We also discussed the importance of notifications in providing real-time updates to clients and how to handle them effectively.

In the next chapter, we'll explain how you can use a low-level server API, as there are some use cases where you might want to do that.

Assignment

For this assignment, we'll again focus on e-commerce. Imagine you have CSV files on the server that need processing. Processing happens when all CSV files on a server are sent one by one as input to a web API. The idea is that this process will be kicked off by calling a tool. Imagine the following program output:

```
Type command> process-files
Notification: info - sales.csv processed
Notification: info - sales.csv processed
Notification: info - sales.csv processed
Files processed: 3
Type command> process-files
Files processed: 0
```

The point of this assignment is to learn how to use notifications. The files can be a list of in-memory entries that get removed as they're processed. You will need to create both a server, where the files to process are, and a client that can process input commands.

Solution

You can access the solution at https://github.com/PacktPublishing/Learn-Model-Context-Protocol-with-Python/blob/main/Chapter05/solutions/README.md.

Quiz

What is the primary benefit of using Streamable HTTP?

- A: It allows for faster access to data
- B: It requires fewer server resources
- C: It is more secure than other protocols

How does Streamable HTTP differ from SSE?

- A: Streamable HTTP uses a text-based format, while SSE uses JSON.
- B: Streamable HTTP can send binary data, while SSE is limited to text.
- C: Streamable HTTP is unidirectional, while SSE is bidirectional.

You can access the solution at https://github.com/PacktPublishing/Learn-Model-Context-Protocol-with-Python/blob/main/Chapter05/solutions/solution-quiz.md.

References

- **Streaming transport**: https://mcp-framework.com/docs/Transports/http-stream-transport/

Unlock this book's exclusive benefits now

UNLOCK NOW

Scan this QR code or go to https://packtpub.com/unlock, then search this book by name.

Note: Keep your purchase invoice ready before you start.

6

Advanced Servers

In *Chapter 3*, you saw how you can build MCP servers. However, there's another way to build these servers – namely, by using a more advanced approach. The reason for using this more advanced approach is that you want to be more in control.

In this chapter, you will learn how to do the following:

- Use context managers to manage the lifecycle of your server
- Improve the architecture of your server
- Understand low-level access to MCP servers

The chapter covers the following topics:

- Why this low-level approach?
- Context managers
- Context managers in MCP servers
- Low-level access
- Organizing your architecture

Why this low-level approach?

At this point, you might be thinking, *Why would I want to do that? The previous approach was so easy!* Well, there are a few reasons why you might want to use this approach. You may want to do the following:

- **Use context managers to manage the lifecycle of your server**: Here, you can do things such as connecting to a database or other services that are connected to your server. By having more control over the lifecycle of your server, you can ensure that your server is properly initialized and cleaned up when it's no longer needed.

- **Improve the architecture of your server**: Having more control over how the server is built allows for more freedom in how tools and resources are registered, but also how incoming requests are handled. This increased control allows you to organize your code in a way that is more maintainable and scalable. This chapter shows you how you can organize your code with both a low-level server and a normal MCP server. It's possible to create a clean architecture in both cases. However, it could be argued that the low-level server approach is a bit cleaner, as you don't have to pass the server instance around. You'll see more about what's meant by that last statement later in this chapter.

- **The only way forward in some cases**: There are cases when you deal with certain features where there simply is no other way forward than a low-level approach. This is true for using *Chapter 9*, on sampling, and *Chapter 10*, on elicitation.

Let's dive into a more low-level approach, so you know what it looks like, so you can choose the approach that suits your project the best.

Context managers

So, what's a context manager to begin with? A **context manager** is a construct that allows you to allocate and release resources precisely when you want to. The most common way to use a context manager is with the `with` statement, which ensures that resources are properly cleaned up after use, even if an error occurs. By using a context manager, your code becomes cleaner and more readable. Let's look at a simple example:

```
with Database_connection() as conn:
    # Use the connection
    result = conn.execute("SELECT * FROM table")
    for row in result:
        print(row)
```

Using contextlib to create context managers

Another way to use context managers is to create a custom context manager using the contextlib (there's a corresponding NPM library called contextlib) module. This allows you to create context managers without defining a class. Here's an example:

```python
import contextlib


@contextlib.contextmanager
def database_connection():
    conn = connect_to_database()
    try:
        yield conn  # This is where the resource is provided to the block
    finally:
        close_connection(conn)  # Cleanup happens here
```

Here, you can see how the DatabaseConnection class is replaced with a database_connection() function that uses the contextlib.contextmanager decorator. The yield statement provides the resource to the block, and the code after the yield statement is executed when the block is exited, ensuring proper cleanup. Is this better than the previous example? Well, at least you type less code.

Implementing a context manager

If you're interested in knowing how to implement a context manager, because you're curious or because you don't want yet another dependency, here's how you can do that:

```python
class DatabaseConnection:
    def __enter__(self):
        self.conn = self.connect_to_database()
        return self.conn

    def __exit__(self, exc_type, exc_value, traceback):
        self.close_connection(self.conn)

    def connect_to_database(self):
        # Logic to connect to the database
        pass
```

```
        def close_connection(self, conn):
            # Logic to close the database connection
            pass
```

In the preceding, the `DatabaseConnection` class implements the context manager protocol by defining the __enter__ and __exit__ methods. The __enter__ method is called when the `with` block is entered, and it returns the resource (in this case, a database connection). The __exit__ method is called when the block is exited, and it handles any cleanup necessary, such as closing the connection. Let's call it like so:

```
    with DatabaseConnection() as conn:
        # Use the connection
        result = conn.execute("SELECT * FROM table")
        for row in result:
            print(row)
```

Without a context manager, your code would look like so:

```
    conn = DatabaseConnection().connect_to_database()
    try:
        # Use the connection
        result = conn.execute("SELECT * FROM table")
        for row in result:
            print(row)
    finally:
        DatabaseConnection().close_connection(conn)
```

Imagine what would happen if you forgot to close the connection in the `finally` block? You might be a very disciplined programmer and always remember to close the connection, but in a larger code base, it's easy to forget. Context managers help you avoid such pitfalls by ensuring that resources are always cleaned up properly.

Let's look at how context managers are used in the context of MCP servers next.

Context managers in MCP servers

MCP allows you to control the lifecycle management of your resources. Let's have a look at some code:

```
    async def load_settings() -> dict:
        """Load settings from a configuration file."""
        # Simulate loading settings
```

```
        return {"setting1": "value1", "setting2": "value2"}


@asynccontextmanager
async def server_lifespan(server: Server) -> AsyncIterator[dict]:
    """Manage server startup and shutdown lifecycle."""
    # Initialize resources on startup
    db = await Database.connect()
    settings = await load_settings()
    try:
        yield {"db": db, "settings": settings}
    finally:
        # Clean up on shutdown
        await db.disconnect()
```

Here, we've done several things:

- Defined an asynchronous context manager, server_lifespan, that manages the lifecycle of the server

- Initialized resources such as a database connection and settings when the server starts, cleaning them up when the server shuts down

- Exposed these resources to the server's request context, allowing handlers to access them easily

Speaking of handlers, let's see how you can access these resources in your server's handlers in the following code:

```
# Pass lifespan to server
server = Server("example-server", lifespan=server_lifespan)


# Access lifespan context in handlers
@server.call_tool()
async def query_db(name: str, arguments: dict) -> list:
    ctx = server.request_context
    db = ctx.lifespan_context["db"]
    settings = ctx.lifespan_context["settings"]
    # TODO: Use the database connection and settings

    return await db.query(arguments["query"])
```

In the preceding code, we've done the following:

- Defined a tool, query_db, that accesses the resources initialized in the server_lifespan context manager.
- Accessed the database connection and settings from the lifespan_context of the server's request context using the db = ctx.lifespan_context["db"] and settings = ctx. lifespan_context["settings"] code.

Great – now we have an understanding of context management and why it exists. Let's look more at low-level access in the next section.

Low-level access

Let's recap how we first build a server so we can easily compare it to how low-level access is different. Here's how you build a simple MCP server with a high-level API:

```python
from mcp.server.fastmcp import FastMCP

mcp = FastMCP("Echo")


@mcp.resource("echo://{message}")
def echo_resource(message: str) -> str:
    """Echo a message as a resource"""
    return f"Resource echo: {message}"


@mcp.tool()
def echo_tool(message: str) -> str:
    """Echo a message as a tool"""
    return f"Tool echo: {message}"
```

The FastMCP class is what you use to instantiate a server – in this case, an instance called mcp. Then we use @mcp to define resources, tools, and prompts.

This is a high-level way of building a server, but what if you want more control over how the server is built? Here's how you can do that using low-level access.

Let's look at how registering features is different. In the past, you would have been used to using decorators associated with specific tools or resources, and so on. What's different in a low-level server is that you need to handle all requests yourself. Instead of handling one tool or resource at a time, you handle all requests related to tools, resources, and prompts in one place.

First, the import is different. See how we import from from `mcp.server.lowlevel` and Server:

```
from mcp.server.lowlevel import Server
```

That's followed by instantiating a server like so:

```
server = Server("low-level-server")
```

Instead of using @mcp.tools() or @mcp.resource(), you register using handlers such as @server. list_tools() and @server.call_tool(). That's a huge difference. The difference lies in that, instead of there being one decorator for every feature, in a low-level server, you respond to all tool requests, whether to call a tool or list tools, resources, or prompts. That means @server. list_tools() is responsible for listing all tools, and you need to implement that logic yourself, whereas a high-level server does that for you. Here's an example of how @server.list_tools() can be implemented:

```
@server.list_tools()
async def handle_list_tools() -> list[types.Tool]:
    tool_list = []
    print(tools)

    for tool in tools.tools.values():
        tool_list.append(
            types.Tool(
                name=tool["name"],
                description=tool["description"],
                inputSchema=tool["input_schema"],
            )
        )
    return tool_list
```

In the preceding code, we've done the following:

- Defined a handler, `handle_list_tools`, that responds to the `list_tools` request.
- Used the `@server.list_tools()` decorator to register this handler with the server.
- Iterated over `tools.tools.values()` to collect all tools and return them in the required format – in this case, a list of `types.Tool` objects. In this case, `tools.tools` is a dictionary that contains all the tools registered with the server that we've created, so it looks something like this:

```
{
    "tools": {
        "echo_tool": {
            "name": "echo_tool",
            "description": "Echo a message as a tool",
            "input_schema": {"type": "object", "properties":
                {"message": {"type": "string"}}}
        }
    }
}
```

Isn't this more work? Well, actually, let's explore in the next section how this could be a great way to organize your code.

Organizing your architecture

A huge advantage of using a low-level server is that you can control the architecture of your server. You can organize your code in a way that makes sense for your project. For example, you can define all your tools in a folder called `tools`. Tools also don't need to know about the server instance. Sounds promising, right? Let's see how next.

> You can organize your code well with a high-level server too, but it's usually a bit messier as you need to pass the server instance around, as we said initially in this chapter.

Here's how you have defined MCP server features so far in a high-level server:

```
from mcp.server.fastmcp import FastMCP

mcp = FastMCP("Echo")
```

```python
@mcp.tool()
def echo_tool(message: str) -> str:
    """Echo a message as a tool"""
    return f"Tool echo: {message}"

@mcp.tool()
def add_tool(a: int, b: int) -> int:
    """Add two numbers as a tool"""
    return a + b

@mcp.tool()
def subtract_tool(a: int, b: int) -> int:
    """Subtract two numbers as a tool"""
    return a - b

@mcp.tool()
def multiply_tool(a: int, b: int) -> int:
    """Multiply two numbers as a tool"""
    return a * b

@mcp.tool()
def divide_tool(a: int, b: int) -> float:
    """Divide two numbers as a tool"""
    if b == 0:
        raise ValueError("Cannot divide by zero")
    return a / b
```

There's nothing wrong with defining a server and its features like the preceding. However, it might be tempting to keep your entry point file relatively empty (save for the server definition) and define all your features in that file. So, you might resort to having a project structure like this:

```
project/
├── server.py
├── tools.py
```

Then your server.py might look like so:

```python
# server.py

from mcp.server.fastmcp import FastMCP
import tools

mcp = FastMCP("Echo")

tools.register_tools(mcp)

# code for running the server
```

Your tools.py might look like so:

```python
from mcp.server.fastmcp import FastMCP

def register_tools(mcp: FastMCP):
    @mcp.tool()
    def echo_tool(message: str) -> str:
        """Echo a message as a tool"""
        return f"Tool echo: {message}"

    @mcp.tool()
    def add_tool(a: int, b: int) -> int:
        """Add two numbers as a tool"""
        return a + b

    @mcp.tool()
    def subtract_tool(a: int, b: int) -> int:
        """Subtract two numbers as a tool"""
        return a - b

    @mcp.tool()
    def multiply_tool(a: int, b: int) -> int:
        """Multiply two numbers as a tool"""
        return a * b

    @mcp.tool()
```

```
    def divide_tool(a: int, b: int) -> float:
        """Divide two numbers as a tool"""
        if b == 0:
            raise ValueError("Cannot divide by zero")
        return a / b
```

You might even have dedicated files for each tool:

```
project/
├── server.py
├── tools/
│   ├── echo.py
│   ├── add.py
│   ├── subtract.py
│   ├── multiply.py
│   └── divide.py
```

So yes, you can organize your code in a way that makes sense for your project. It's hard to get away from having to pass the server instance. It should be said that the high-level server does provide a `create_tool()` function that allows you to create tools without you having to use the `@mcp.tool()` decorator. However, and this is the opinion of the author, it's just easier to use the low-level server for this purpose. Let's look at how you can do this in the next section.

Constructing a list tools response in a low-level server

So, let's see whether low-level access can help improve our architecture further. The goal is to have a server that can register tools, resources, and prompts in a way that is easy to maintain and extend.

So, we said the following so far about the low-level server:

- Instead of using `FastMCP`, you use the `Server` class from `mcp.server.lowlevel`
- You can register features using handlers such as `@server.list_tools()` and `@server.call_tool()` to handle listing all tools and handling all tool calls

Let's study these handlers in more detail and how we can construct them, to see how we can leverage them:

```
@server.list_tools()
async def handle_list_tools() -> list[types.Tool]:
    tool_list = []
```

```
        tool_list.append(
            types.Tool(
                name=tool["name"],
                description=tool["description"],
                inputSchema=tool["input_schema"],
            )
        )

        return tool_list
```

Here, we observe that the return type is a list of types.Tool objects. This is reflected in the code, where we append a types.Tool object to tool_list like so:

```
    tool_list.append(
        types.Tool(
            name=tool["name"],
            description=tool["description"],
            inputSchema=tool["input_schema"],
        )
    )
```

Organizing your code and creating tools and schemas

Now that we know how to register tools, let's see how we can organize the code a bit. The goal is to achieve the following:

- A file for each tool, so we can easily manage the code
- Register all the tools in one place

Sounds like a great goal, right? Who doesn't want maintainability? Let's create a folder structure like so:

```
server.py
tools/
├── __init__.py
├── add.py
```

What we're seeing here is that we have a server.py file that will be the entry point of our server, and a tools/ folder that contains all the tools. The tools/init.py file is used to register to collect all the tools, and server.py and @mcp.list_tools() will be used to register all the tools. Let's look at __init__.py first:

```
from .add import tool_add

tools = {
    tool_add["name"] : tool_add
}
```

That looks super simple – just a dictionary that imports the tool_add function from the add.py file and adds it to the tools dictionary. Now let's look at the add.py file:

```
# add.py

from .schema import AddInputModel

async def add_handler(args) -> float:

    try:
        # Validate input using Pydantic model
        input_model = AddInputModel(**args)
    except Exception as e:
        raise ValueError(f"Invalid input: {str(e)}")

    # TODO: add Pydantic, so we can create an AddInputModel and validate
    args

    """Handler function for the add tool."""
    return float(input_model.a) + float(input_model.b)

tool_add = {
    "name": "add",
    "description": "Adds two numbers",
    "input_schema": AddInputModel,
    "handler": add_handler
}
```

In the preceding code, we've done the following:

- Imported `AddInputModel` and added that as `input_schema`
- Defined an `add_handler` function that takes the arguments and returns their sum
- Created a `tool_add` dictionary that contains the tool's name, description, input schema, and handler function

As you can see, there are no imports to anything MCP, and it therefore looks pretty clean.

Finally, let's look at the `schema.py` file:

```python
from pydantic import BaseModel


class AddInputModel(BaseModel):
    a: float
    b: float
```

Here we're using the **Pydantic** library to define input models. We can extend this file with new types as we add more tools to our solution.

Handling a tool being called

So far, you've seen how we're able to take care of a call asking us to list all the tools. But there's another case we need to handle, namely when a client is trying to call a tool. For that, we need to do the following with the incoming tool calling request:

- Identify which tool to call.
- Parse out the arguments and, in doing so, also validate them. This is where our Pydantic schemas will come in handy to help us with this.

Let's start with the request on the server:

```python
# server.py


@server.call_tool()
async def handle_call_tool(
    name: str, arguments: dict[str, str] | None
) -> list[types.TextContent]:
    pass
```

Note how we need to refer to the `@server.call_tool` decorator and that the return type needs to be `list[types.TextContext]`.

Next, let's see if we can identify the correct tool:

```python
# server.py
if name not in tools.tools:
    raise ValueError(f"Unknown tool: {name}")


tool = tools.tools[name]
```

Okay, let's get ready to call a handler on the tool and construct a response to the calling client:

```python
# server.py


try:
    result = await tool["handler"](arguments)
except Exception as e:
    raise ValueError(f"Error calling tool {name}: {str(e)}")


return [
    types.TextContent(type="text", text=str(result))
]
```

Note how we invoke the `handler` property on the `tool` object with `arguments` as a parameter. What does the handler look like on the tool, though, and how does it work?

```python
# add.py
from .schema import AddInputModel


async def add_handler(args) -> float:

    try:
        # Validate input using Pydantic model
        input_model = AddInputModel(**args)
    except Exception as e:
        raise ValueError(f"Invalid input: {str(e)}")


    print (f"Adding {args['a']} and {args['b']}")
    """Handler function for the add tool."""
    return float(args['a']) + float(args['b'])
```

Here, we use a try-catch to pass args into the AddInputModel class. It takes a dictionary, and by passing it as **args, we're unpacking the dictionary into keyword arguments. If the input is invalid, ValueError is raised, with a message indicating what went wrong. This way, you can ensure that the input to your tool is always valid and meets the expected schema.

Great, we've now managed to handle both listing all tools and calling a specific tool while also ensuring some validation of input arguments takes place.

I'm sure you could improve this setup further, but this is a lot better than what we started with.

Summary

In this chapter, you learned how to use the low-level server to create a more maintainable architecture for your MCP server. You saw how to register tools, handle requests, and validate input using schemas. This approach allows you to easily add new tools and manage existing ones, making your server more flexible and easier to maintain.

In our next chapter, we'll cover how to build clients that can interact with our MCP servers.

Assignment

Let's see if we can organize the e-commerce server that we created in *Chapter 3*. Here's the code for reference. Create a tools directory – use Pydantic and a low-level API.

```python
# server.py
from mcp.server.fastmcp import FastMCP
import uuid

# Create an MCP server
mcp = FastMCP("Demo")

class Customer:
    def __init__(self,id: int, name: str, email: str):
        self.id = id
        self.name = name
        self.email = email

class Category:
    def __init__(self, name: str, description: str):
        self.id = uuid.uuid4()
```

```python
            self.name = name
            self.description = description


class Product:
    def __init__(self, name: str, price: float, description: str):
        self.name = name
        self.price = price
        self.description = description


class CartItem:
    def __init__(self, cart_id: int, product_id: int, quantity: int):
        if cart_id != 0:
            self.cart_id = cart_id
        else:
            self.cart_id = uuid.uuid4()
        self.product_id = product_id
        self.quantity = quantity


class Cart:
    def __init__(self, cart_id: int, customer_id: int):
        if cart_id != 0:
            self.cart_id = cart_id
        else:
            self.cart_id = uuid.uuid4()
        self.customer_id = customer_id


class Order:
    def __init__(self, order_id: int, customer_id: int):
        if order_id != 0:
            self.order_id = order_id
        else:
            self.order_id = uuid.uuid4()
        self.customer_id = customer_id


products = [
    Product("Product 1", 10.0, "Description of Product 1"),
    Product("Product 2", 20.0, "Description of Product 2"),
```

```
        Product("Product 3", 30.0, "Description of Product 3")
    ]


    orders = [
        Order(1, 101),
        Order(0, 101),
        Order(0, 102)
    ]


    carts = []
    customers = [
        Customer(1, "Customer 1", "email")
    ]



    categories = [
        Category("Category 1", "Description of Category 1"),
        Category("Category 2", "Description of Category 2"),
        Category("Category 3", "Description of Category 3")
    ]


    product_catalog = [
        {
            "name": "Product 1",
            "price": 10.0,
            "description": "Description of Product 1",
            "category_id": 1
        },
        {
            "name": "Product 2",
            "price": 20.0,
            "description": "Description of Product 2",
            "category_id": 2
        },
        {
            "name": "Product 3",
            "price": 30.0,
```

```
            "description": "Description of Product 3",
            "category_id": 3
        }
]


# get orders
@mcp.tool()
def get_orders(customer_id:int = 0) -> [Order]:
    """get all orders"""

    if customer_id != 0 and not any(customer.id == customer_id for
        customer in customers):
        raise ValueError(f"Invalid customer_id: {customer_id}")

    filtered_orders = orders
    if customer_id != 0:
        filtered_orders = [order for order in orders if order.customer_id
            == customer_id]

    return [{"type": "text", "name": f"ID: {order.order_id},customer:
        {order.customer_id}"} for order in filtered_orders]

# get order by id
@mcp.tool()
def get_order(order_id:int) -> Order:
    """get order by id"""
    for order in orders:
        if order.order_id == order_id:
            return {"type": "text", "name": f"ID: {order.order_
                id},customer: {order.customer_id}"}
    return None

# place order
@mcp.tool()
def place_order(customer_id:int) -> Order:
    """place order"""
```

```python
    if customer_id != 0 and not any(customer.id == customer_id for
        customer in customers):
        raise ValueError(f"Invalid customer_id: {customer_id}")


    new_order = Order(0, customer_id)
    orders.append(new_order)
    return {"type": "text", "name": f"ID: {new_order.order_id},customer:
        {new_order.customer_id}"}


# get carts
@mcp.tool()
def get_cart(customer_id:int) -> [Cart]:
    """get a singular cart"""


    if customer_id != 0 and not any(customer.id == customer_id for
        customer in customers):
        raise ValueError(f"Invalid customer_id: {customer_id}")


    cart = next((cart for cart in carts if cart.customer_id == customer_
        id), None)
    if cart:
        return {"type": "text", "name": f"ID: {cart.cart_id},customer:
            {cart.customer_id}"}
    else:
        return None


# get cart items
@mcp.tool()
def get_cart_items(cart_id:int) -> [CartItem]:
    """get cart items"""
    cart_items = [item for item in carts if item.cart_id == cart_id]
    return [{"type": "text", "name": f"ID: {item.cart_id},product: {item.
        product_id},quantity: {item.quantity}"} for item in cart_items]


# add to cart
@mcp.tool()
def add_to_cart(cart_id:int, product_id:int, quantity:int) -> CartItem:
    """add to cart"""
```

```python
        new_cart_item = CartItem(cart_id, product_id, quantity)
        carts.append(new_cart_item)
        return {"type": "text", "name": f"ID: {new_cart_item.cart_id},product:
            {new_cart_item.product_id},quantity: {new_cart_item.quantity}"}


# tool, all products
@mcp.tool()
def get_all_products() -> [Product]:
    """Get all products"""
    return [{"type": "text", "name": f"ID: {product.name},price: {product.
        price},description: {product.description}"} for product in products]


# tool, product by id
@mcp.tool()
def get_product(product_id: int) -> Product:
    """Get product by ID"""
    for product in products:
        if product.name == product_id:
            return {"type": "text", "name": f"ID: {product.name},price:
                {product.price},description: {product.description}"}
    return None


# tool, all categories
@mcp.tool()
def get_all_categories() -> [Category]:
    """Get all categories"""
    return [{"type": "text", "name": f"ID: {category.name},description:
        {category.description}"} for category in categories]


# tool, all customers
@mcp.tool()
def get_all_customers() -> [Customer]:
    """Get all customers"""
    return [{"type": "text", "name": f"ID: {customer.id},name: {customer.
        name},email: {customer.email}"} for customer in customers]
```

Solution

You can access the solution at `https://github.com/PacktPublishing/Learn-Model-Context-Protocol-with-Python/blob/main/Chapter06/solutions/README.md`.

Quiz

What are some benefits of using a low-level server?

- A: You use less memory
- B: You have better control over how requests are processed
- C: You can define your own transports

You can access the solution at `https://github.com/PacktPublishing/Learn-Model-Context-Protocol-with-Python/blob/main/Chapter06/solutions/solution-quiz.md`.

Unlock this book's exclusive benefits now   **UNLOCK NOW**

Scan this QR code or go to `https://packtpub.com/unlock`,
then search this book by name.

Note: Keep your purchase invoice ready before you start.

7

Building Clients

To consume an MCP server, you need some form of client. You could, for example, use an application such as **Claude Desktop** or **Virtual Studio Code** (**VS Code**), as they have the ability to consume MCP servers and will handle the discovery of features and be able to use them. There are also cases where you want your own written client. A good example of this situation is when you want to build in AI capabilities as part of your app. Imagine, for example, that you have an e-commerce app and want to have an AI-improved search. The MCP server would be a separate app, whereas the client would be built into the e-commerce app.

With this in mind, let's explore how we can build a client and what goes into it.

In this chapter, you will learn how to do the following:

- Build a client using both STDIO and SSE transports
- Consume an MCP server and its features
- Leverage an LLM to enhance your client experience

The chapter covers the following topics:

- Building a client
- Exercise: Building a client
- Clients with LLMs
- Working with an LLM
- Exercise: Integrating the LLM

Building a client

So, what goes into building a client? At a mile-high level, here's what we need to do:

1. Set up the client to connect to the server.

2. List features.

3. Select a feature to use.

4. Prompt the user for parameters.

5. Present the results.

Great, now that we understand the high-level steps, let's see if we can build it next in an exercise that you're welcome to code along with.

Exercise: Building a client

In this exercise, you will build a client that connects to the server and consumes its features. You will use the SDK to build the client and call the server. The client will be a simple command-line application that allows you to select a feature and provide its parameters. The client will then call the server and display the results.

Set up the client to connect to the server

Let's first create the client code needed to establish a connection to the server:

```python
from mcp import ClientSession, StdioServerParameters, types
from mcp.client.stdio import stdio_client

# Create server parameters for stdio connection
server_params = StdioServerParameters(
    command="mcp",  # Executable
    args=["run", "server.py"],  # Optional command line arguments
    env=None,  # Optional environment variables
)

async def run():
    async with stdio_client(server_params) as (read, write):
        async with ClientSession(
            read, write
```

```
        ) as session:
            # Initialize the connection
            await session.initialize()

            # list features

if __name__ == "__main__":
    import asyncio

    asyncio.run(run())
```

In the preceding code, we've done the following:

- Created a `StdioServerParameters` object that specifies the command to run the server and any optional command-line arguments. Why we do this is because the server will be run at the same time as the client, so we need to specify how to run it.

- Defined a run function that creates a `ClientSession` object and initializes the connection to the server. Inside the run function, we will soon add the code to list and call features.

List features

So far, we've set up the client to connect to the server. Now, let's add the code to list the features available on the server. This is done differently depending on the type of feature. Let's add some code:

```
# List available resources
resources = await session.list_resources()
print("LISTING RESOURCES")
for resource in resources:
    print("Resource: ", resource)

# List available tools
tools = await session.list_tools()
print("LISTING TOOLS")
for tool in tools.tools:
    print("Tool: ", tool.name)
```

There, we have the following code to list the features:

- `List available resources`: This lists all the resources available on the server. We also print the resource name to the console.
- `List available tools`: This lists all the tools available in the server, and we print the tool name to the console. We could also print the tool description and input schema, but for now, we just print the name.

Select a feature to use

Let's show how to use our listed features by taking one of the tools and calling it. In this case, we will use the add tool that we created in the previous chapter. The add tool takes two parameters, a and b, and returns the sum of the two numbers. However, imagine now the user has been presented with a list of tools and chosen a tool. Let's now prompt the user for the parameters needed to call the tool:

```
# Read information from the first tool
tool_name = tools.tools[0].name
print(f"Using tool: {tool_name}")
first_value = input("Enter first value: ")
second_value = input("Enter second value: ")

# Call a tool
print("CALL TOOL")
result = await session.call_tool(tool_name, arguments={
    "a": first_value, "b": second_value})
print(result.content)
```

In the preceding code, we've done the following:

- Read the name of the first tool in the list and printed it to the console.
- Prompted the user for the first and second value to use as parameters for the tool.
- Called the tool using the `call_tool` method and passed the parameters as a dictionary. The result is printed to the console.

Great, now we have a client that can connect to the server, list the features, and call a tool. However, this is still quite programmatic and not very user-friendly.

The full code

Before we move on to integrate an LLM, let's show the complete code for the client:

```python
from mcp import ClientSession, StdioServerParameters, types
from mcp.client.stdio import stdio_client


# Create server parameters for stdio connection
server_params = StdioServerParameters(
    command="mcp",  # Executable
    args=["run", "server.py"],  # Optional command line arguments
    env=None,  # Optional environment variables
)


async def run():
    async with stdio_client(server_params) as (read, write):
        async with ClientSession(
            read, write
        ) as session:
            # Initialize the connection
            await session.initialize()

            # List available resources
            resources = await session.list_resources()
            print("LISTING RESOURCES")
            for resource in resources:
                print("Resource: ", resource)

            # List available tools
            tools = await session.list_tools()
            print("LISTING TOOLS")
            for tool in tools.tools:
                print("Tool: ", tool.name)

            # Read information from the first tool
            tool_name = tools.tools[0].name
```

```
            print(f"Using tool: {tool_name}")
            first_value = input("Enter first value: ")
            second_value = input("Enter second value: ")

             # Call a tool
            print("CALL TOOL")
            result = await session.call_tool(tool_name, arguments={"a":
                first_value, "b": second_value})
            print(result.content)

            # Read a resource
            print("READING RESOURCE")
            content, mime_type = await session.read_resource("greeting://
                hello")


    if __name__ == "__main__":
        import asyncio

        asyncio.run(run())
```

Okay, if you typed along with the code, you should now have a working client that can connect to the server and consume its features. You will get an additional chance to practice this in the assignment at the end of this chapter.

Let's improve the client next by integrating an LLM into it. You will get to see how this offers a better user experience and how it can be used to abstract away the complexity of using the server.

Clients with LLMs

So far, you've seen how you can build and test a client using STDIO and SSE. However, you might have noticed how this approach is quite programmatic and not very user-friendly. That is, for each capability you want to use, you need to know the exact name of the feature and its parameters. This is where LLMs come in. By involving an LLM in the client, you can abstract away the *knowing* part and instead focus on the *doing* part. Here's how it works.

Before using an LLM

Here's how you would build an app without an LLM and how the flow in the app would be:

1. List server features.

2. The user selects a feature and the client asks for the parameters.

3. Do something with the response.

This approach is quite rigid and requires the user to explicitly know and select one of the features listed. So, what's better?

After involving an LLM

To address clients that feel rigid, imagine instead that the user doesn't know about the features; they only communicate with prompts. With that thought in mind, now let's look at the flow of the app:

1. List server features.

2. Convert the list of features into an LLM tool.

3. The user types a natural language request.

4. The client sends the request to the LLM, which figures out which feature to use and what parameters to send, and if there's no matching feature, responds with a generic LLM response.

The difference in user experience is quite significant. This second approach means the user no longer needs to know about the features, and doesn't need to select features to use. Instead, the user can just type a natural language request, and the LLM will figure out the rest.

Let's see how this works in practice.

Working with an LLM

There are many AI providers out there that let you call an LLM. In this book, we will use **GitHub Models**, as that's a free option, and all you need to use it is a GitHub account. To use GitHub Models, you will either need to start your project in GitHub Codespaces or set up a **personal access token (PAT)** with the right permissions. The reason you need a token in the first place is that you are calling an API, and the token is used as a bearer token to authenticate the request. To use a local AI model via, for example, **Ollama**, you wouldn't need a token. You can type the token directly in the source code, but it's recommended to keep it in an environment variable for security reasons.

So, what do we need to know if we've never worked with AI before? Well, the idea is to send in a prompt and get back a response. The prompt is natural language text that describes what you want the LLM to do. The response is also natural language text that contains the answer to your prompt.

To use LLM in combination with MCP, however, the idea is to have the LLM indicate which functions to call given a specific prompt. For example, with the prompt Add 1 and 2, the LLM should indicate that the add function should be called with the parameters a=1 and b=2, if we have defined an add function in the MCP server with that name and parameters.

Here's what the calling code looks like. In the following code, we will be calling a GitHub model, so make sure you have a GitHub account and have created a PAT with the right permissions, or start it in GitHub Codespaces.

What's important to define is the following:

- The endpoint for GitHub Models
- The model to use – in this case, gpt-4o
- The prompt to send in – you can collect this data from a user input or hardcode it, as in the following example
- The functions to use – in this case, we will be using the add tool that we created in the previous chapter

It's entirely possible to just send a prompt and get a response back, but in this case, we want the LLM to indicate which function to call, so we will be sending in a function definition as well. A **function definition** is a JSON object that describes the function name, description, and parameters. The parameters are defined using JSON schema.

```
# json description of functions
functions = [
    {
        "type": "function",
        "function": {
            "name": "add",
            "description": "Add two numbers",
            "type": "function",
            "parameters": {
                "type": "object",
                "properties": {
                    "a": {
```

```
                              "type": "number",
                              "description": "The first number to add"
                          },
                          "b": {
                              "type": "number",
                              "description": "The second number to add"
                          }
                      },
                      "required": ["a", "b"]
                  }
              }
          }
]


# get token from environment variable
token = os.environ["GITHUB_TOKEN"]

# the endpoint for GitHub Models
endpoint = "https://models.github.ai/inference"

# the model to use
model_name = "gpt-4o"

# creation of chat client
client = OpenAI(
    base_url=endpoint,
    api_key=token
)
print("CALLING LLM")
response = client.chat.completions.create(
    messages=[
        {
            "role": "system",
            "content": "You are a helpful assistant.",
        },
        {
            "role": "user",
```

```
            "content": prompt,
        },
    ],
    model=model_name,
    tools = functions,
    # Optional parameters
    temperature=1.,
    max_tokens=1000,
    top_p=1.
)

response_message = response.choices[0].message
print("LLM RESPONSE: ", response_message)
```

It's worth mentioning though that, additionally to prompts, you can also send in configuration to the LLM, such as `temperature`, `max_tokens`, and top p. We won't dive into what these parameters mean – you can read more about them in the OpenAI documentation – but in short, they control the randomness and creativity of the LLM response and also the size of what's known as the context window.

Exercise: Integrating the LLM

So, let's see how we can integrate an LLM into the client. The goal is to have a much better user experience and to abstract away the complexity of using the server. To get there, we will need to take the following steps:

1. **List server features**: By listing the features, we can see what we have available to us

2. **Convert the list of features to an LLM tool**: The features from the MCP server are not directly usable by the LLM, so we need to convert them into a format that the LLM can understand

3. **Manage user input**: This will allow the user to type a natural language request and the LLM on our client will make a completion request, and in doing so, tell us which feature to use and what parameters to send.

Let's do this!

List server features

You might be building this client as the first thing you do if you, for example, are consuming someone else's MCP server. In that case, make sure you install the MCP SDK before proceeding.

The first step is no different from what we did before. We need to list the features available on the server. This is done by a call to listing tools, like so:

```
tools = await session.list_tools()
print("LISTING TOOLS")
for tool in tools.tools:
    print("Tool: ", tool.name)
```

Convert the list of features into an LLM tool

Our next step is important, as we're going to convert the list of features into a format that the LLM can understand. This will set us up for the next step, where we will use the LLM to figure out which feature to use. Here's the conversion code:

1. Let's add the conversion code function:

    ```
    def to_llm_tool(tool):
        tool_schema = {
            "type": "function",
            "function": {
                "name": tool.name,
                "description": tool.description,
                "type": "function",
                "parameters": {
                    "type": "object",
                    "properties": tool.inputSchema["properties"]
                }
            }
        }

        return tool_schema
    ```

    The preceding code defines a function that takes a tool as input and converts it into a format that the LLM can understand.

2. Let's call the conversion code:

```
functions = []

for tool in tools.tools:
    print("Tool: ", tool.name)
    print("Tool", tool.inputSchema["properties"])
    functions.append(to_llm_tool(tool))
```

From the code, you can see that we loop through the tools' response and call the conversion code for each tool.

Great, now we are well set up for using the LLM. The next step is to manage user input and send a completion request to the LLM. In the response from the LLM, the LLM will tell us which function to use and what parameters. In this case, the function to call will be a feature on the server.

The user types a natural language request and the LLM makes a completion request

Let's look at how we can call the LLM now that we have tools for it to use.

There are two parts to this: the first part is to call the LLM, and the second part is to learn whether the LLM has returned a function call or a generic response.

1. Make the LLM call:

```
def call_llm(prompt, functions):
    token = os.environ["GITHUB_TOKEN"]
    endpoint = "https://models.github.ai/inference"

    model_name = "gpt-4o"

    client = OpenAI(
        base_url=endpoint,
        api_key=token,
    )

    print("CALLING LLM")
    response = client.complete(
        messages=[
            {
```

```
                "role": "system",
                "content": "You are a helpful assistant.",
            },
            {
                "role": "user",
                "content": prompt,
            },
        ],
        model=model_name,
        tools = functions,
        # Optional parameters
        temperature=1.,
        max_tokens=1000,
        top_p=1.
    )

    response_message = response.choices[0].message
    print("LLM RESPONSE: ", response_message)

    functions_to_call = []
```

In the preceding code, we've done the following:

- Created a function that takes a prompt and the list of functions as input and returns the LLM response.
- Called the LLM using the complete method and passed the prompt and functions as parameters. The response is printed to the console.

2. Let's check whether the LLM returned a function call by adding the following code:

```
    if response_message.tool_calls:
        for tool_call in response_message.tool_calls:
            print("TOOL: ", tool_call)
            name = tool_call.function.name
            args = json.loads(tool_call.function.arguments)
            functions_to_call.append({ "name": name, "args": args })

    return functions_to_call
```

In the preceding code, we've done the following:

- Checked whether the LLM returned a function call by checking whether the tool_ calls property is present in the response message
- Looped through the tool_calls and printed the tool name and arguments to the console
- Returned the list of functions to call

The client figures out which server feature to use and what parameters to send

At this point, we have the LLM response, and it even returns which functions to call, if any. The next step is to check the functions to call and call the MCP server if needed:

```
functions_to_call = call_llm(prompt, functions)

# call suggested functions
for f in functions_to_call:
    result = await session.call_tool(f["name"], arguments=f["args"])
    print("TOOLS result: ", result.content)
```

In the preceding code, we've done the following:

- Called the LLM and got the functions to call.
- Looped through the functions to call and called the MCP server using the call_tool method. The result is printed to the console.

Nice, right? The user is surely thanking you now for making their life easier, as they can use natural language to interact with the server.

Summary

In this chapter, we've explored how to build clients that can connect to an MCP server and consume its features. We started by building a simple client that could list and call features on the server. We then improved the client by integrating an LLM, which allowed us to create a much better user experience by enabling natural language interactions with the server.

In the next chapter, we will explore how to consume an MCP server using VS Code and Claude for desktop.

Assignment

For this assignment, you will once again focus on e-commerce. You will build an experience where the user can interact with an e-commerce server:

- Ask for products of a certain category
- Add products to the cart, all done using natural language

Solution

Here's a solution for a client. It covers both clients with and without an LLM.

You can access the solution at `https://github.com/PacktPublishing/Learn-Model-Context-Protocol-with-Python/blob/main/Chapter07/solutions/README.md`.

Quiz

What can a client access on an MCP server?

- A: Prompts, tools, and resources
- B: Tools, prompts, and services
- C: Tools and prompts

What's the benefit of adding an LLM to your client?

- A: It's better to place the LLM on the server
- B: It makes the client faster
- C: An LLM on the client allows the end user to use prompts to interact with the server, which makes for a much better user experience

You can access the solution at `https://github.com/PacktPublishing/Learn-Model-Context-Protocol-with-Python/blob/main/Chapter07/solutions/solution-quiz.md`.

References

- **Model Context Protocol**: `https://modelcontextprotocol.io/introduction`
- **Build clients**: `https://modelcontextprotocol.io/quickstart/client`
- **Python SDK**: `https://github.com/modelcontextprotocol/python-sdk`

Unlock this book's exclusive benefits now

UNLOCK NOW

Scan this QR code or go to `https://packtpub.com/unlock`, then search this book by name.

Note: Keep your purchase invoice ready before you start.

8

Consuming Servers

So far, we have looked at how to create servers, but also at consuming them via bespoke clients that you have to write yourself. In this section, we will look at how to consume servers using existing software, such as **Visual Studio Code (VS Code)** or **Claude Desktop**. When we say *consume*, what we mean is installing servers, configuring them, and then using them to run tools or interact with the server in some way.

In this chapter, you will learn how to do the following:

- Understand how to consume servers using existing tools
- Install and configure servers in VS Code
- Work with the mcp.json file for server management
- Manage secrets and configuration for servers
- Use VS Code to test and interact with servers
- Apply security best practices when consuming servers

The chapter covers the following topics:

- Consuming with hosts such as Claude Desktop and VS Code
- Installation process
- Adding a server
- Local and global install
- Tips and tricks
- Security aspects
- Suggestion for servers

Consuming with hosts such as Claude Desktop and VS Code

Consuming servers, okay, what does that mean? So to use an MCP server and its features, you need a way to interact with it. You've seen in *Chapter 7* how to create a server and how to write a client that can interact with it. That's a perfectly valid way to consume a server, but it requires you to write code.

Another approach is to use existing software such as Claude Desktop or VS Code. These tools are designed to work with MCP servers, and they also provide a large language model that ensures that you can interact with the server in a more user-friendly way via prompts.

We think of these two pieces of software as hosts, as they have a built-in MCP client, but they also use configuration files to keep track of the servers that are installed, the tools that are available, and so on.

How do they work? Well, they work in the following way:

- Initiate a connection to the MCP server through a selected transport type, such as STDIO, SSE, or Streamable HTTP
- Provide a user interface to interact with the server and let you type prompts, interact with tools, configuration, and more
- Use configuration files to keep track of installed servers, available tools, and other settings

Here's an example of the user interface in VS Code, which is representative of how these hosts work:

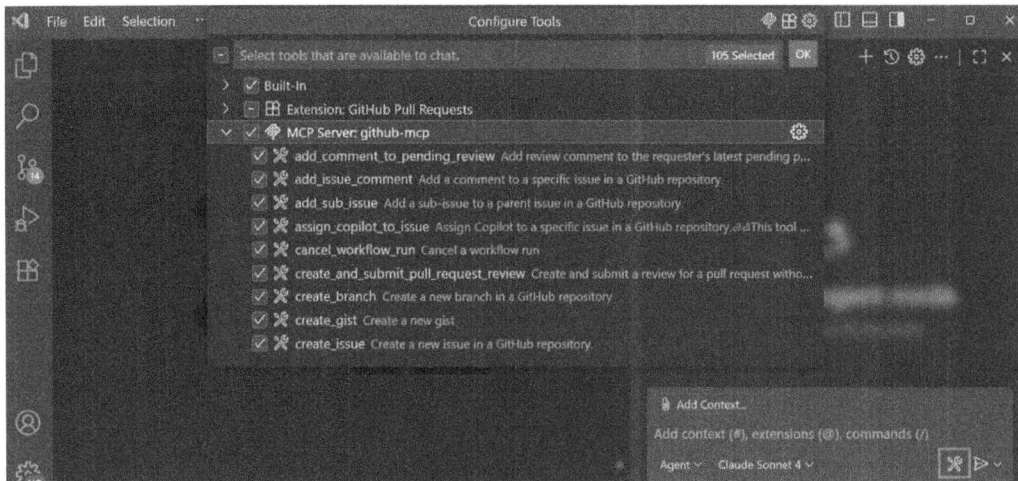

Figure 8.1 – VS Code interface

In the preceding figure, you can see the following:

- A list of tools currently available via servers that are installed

- A chat interface where you can type prompts

Let's talk about specific hosts next and their features.

MCP support in VS Code

VS Code, together with GitHub Copilot, has extensive support for MCP servers. There are a variety of features that help you to install, configure, and secure servers. It supports use cases such as trying out servers you are building, as well as turning VS Code into an agentic app that can run tools through your prompts.

Here's a list of features that VS Code provides for MCP servers:

- **Installing servers**: VS Code lets you install servers both on a global level and on a workspace level. It supports the three transport types: STDIO, SSE, and Streamable HTTP.

- **Managing tools**: You can enable and disable tools for a server, which is useful to ensure that the client has the context it needs.

- **Interacting with features**: In addition to tools, it also supports features such as user prompts and resources.

- **Managing servers**: You can add and remove servers and configure them.

- **Sampling**: It supports sampling, which means that when a server sends a sample request, you can interact with it and tweak the request before sending back a response.

- **Elicitations**: It also supports elicitation requests, which are scenarios when the server needs more information from the user to proceed with a request.

- **Logging and debugging**: There's also support for logging and debugging, which is useful when you are developing servers or clients.

Additional features are being made available all the time, and you're recommended to use **VS Code Insiders** if you want to try these features as early as possible, as they're shipped there first.

Claude Desktop

You can also use Claude Desktop to consume MCP servers. Head over to the download page (`https://claude.ai/download`) to install a client for your operating system. Just like VS Code, it provides a user interface and a whole set of features to interact with MCP servers.

Claude does a lot more than just work with MCP servers; it's a fully-fledged AI assistant and is perhaps best compared with similar products such as ChatGPT or Copilot. For a full set of features, head over to this page: `https://claude.ai/login?returnTo=%2F%3F#features`.

Installation process

To install servers, there's a central concept for both Claude and VS Code, namely, the `mcp.json` file. This file is your main configuration file where you add information on where the servers are and additional configuration needed. In fact, this JSON file acts like a manifest file for what servers are installed. The act of installing a file means adding an entry to this file. Here's an example of an `mcp.json` file:

```
{
    "inputs": [

    ],
    "servers": {
        "docs": {
            "type": "http",
            "url": "https://learn.microsoft.com/api/mcp"
        }
    }
}
```

💡 **Quick tip:** Enhance your coding experience with the **AI Code Explainer** and **Quick Copy** features. Open this book in the next-gen Packt Reader. Click the **Copy** button (1) to quickly copy code into your coding environment, or click the **Explain** button (2) to get the AI assistant to explain a block of code to you.

```
                                                    Copy      Explain
function calculate(a, b) {
    return {sum: a + b};                              1           2
};
```

💡 🔒 **The next-gen Packt Reader** is included for free with the purchase of this book. Scan the QR code OR go to `https://packtpub.com/unlock`, then use the search bar to find this book by name. Double-check the edition shown to make sure you get the right one.

In this file, we have a `servers` attribute with one server entry to `https://learn.microsoft.com/api/mcp`; this MCP server is now considered installed.

The full installation process for installing and running a feature on a server looks like so:

1. Install a server by adding an entry `mcp.json` file in the `servers` attribute.
2. Start the server.
3. Use the server by typing a prompt matching a tool in the server.

We'll explore such a scenario later in this chapter, but now you have a mile-high understanding of it. Let's go into more depth on the `mcp.json` file.

The mcp.json file

The mcp.json file has two primary attributes:

- inputs: This is used for defining placeholders for sensitive information, such as API keys or tokens. The idea is that you define that you want an input prompt to appear, and the answer should be stored in a variable that you can later refer to. Here's an example of this:

```
[
    {
        "id": "my_api_key",
        "description": "The API key that my MCP server needs",
        "type": "promptString",
        "password": true
    }
]
```

By the preceding definition, the user interface in VS Code will start an input prompt asking you to fill in this information. This then needs to be paired with a server entry, like so:

```
"my_mcp_server": {
    "type": "http",
    "url": "http://localhost:8000/mcp",
    "headers": {
        "Authorization": "Bearer ${my_api_key}"
    }
}
```

Note how my_api_key is now passed in as a header property so that every time we call "http://localhost:8000/mcp", it will also pass the API key, ensuring that we can access our MCP server securely. Setting things up this way ensures that secrets stay out of mcp.json.

- servers: This property takes a JSON object with server entries. What you need to know is that these entries look different depending on which transport is being used by the server. Let's show examples for each transport type:

  - **Using Streamable HTTP:**

    ```
    "my_mcp_server": {
        "type": "http",
    ```

```
            "url": "http://localhost:8000/mcp"
      }
```

In this case, it's using Streamable HTTP; we can see that as the type value is http and a url value is specified. Let's look at SSE next.

- **SSE:**

```
"my_mcp_server": {
    "type": "sse",
    "url": "http://localhost:8000/sse"
}
```

SSE, just like Streamable HTTP, is a transport meant for servers that are accessed remotely. Therefore, a url value is used in both cases to point out where these servers live.

- **STDIO:**

```
"playwright": {
    "command": "npx",
    "args": ["-y", "@executeautomation/playwright-mcp-
server"]
}
```

STDIO, or **standard I/O**, needs to specify a command and args property as it needs to point out how to start the server in question. It's not needed for SSE or Streamable HTTP, as these servers live remotely.

Adding a server

You've already seen in the previous section how various servers can be added, but let's go through the motions of adding and using a server. Let's use **Playwright**, an **end-to-end (E2E)** testing framework, as an example. To install it as an MCP server, what you usually do for any server is to locate its GitHub repo and see what its installation instructions are. For Playwright, its repository is here: https://github.com/microsoft/playwright-mcp.

There are quite a lot of instructions as this server offers a lot of features, but let's grab the installation instructions from its *Getting started* section, which looks like so:

```
"playwright": {
    "command": "npx",
```

```
    "args": [
    "@playwright/mcp@latest"
    ]
}
```

Here, we see how it's clearly a STDIO type server as its command and args properties are populated.

Step 1: Installing the server

Let's install this via VS Code. By doing so, we have a couple of different options on how to install it:

- Add the entry directly to an mcp.json file.
- Use a user interface, either with the **Add Server** button that's present when you view the mcp.json file or by running the MCP: Add Server command from the command palette. In both cases, it will trigger a user interface asking you to decide on what transport to use, and either url or command and args information, depending on the chosen transport.

As an example, let's click **Add Server**; you should be presented with the following interface:

Choose the type of MCP server to add	
Command (stdio) Run a local command that implements the MCP protocol	Manual Install
HTTP (HTTP or Server-Sent Events) Connect to a remote HTTP server that implements the MCP protocol	
NPM Package Install from an NPM package name	Model-Assisted
Pip Package Install from a Pip package name	
Docker Image Install from a Docker image	
Browse MCP Servers...	

Figure 8.2 – Installing the server

As you can see, there are numerous options for installing a server: different transports, some also from different package managers, and even Docker.

In fact, if you choose the **Browse MCP Servers...** option, it will take you to a list of vetted MCP servers (https://code.visualstudio.com/insider/mcp) and let you choose a server from there.

We have the complete instructions for working with Playwright from its GitHub repo, but let's install from this list of servers by selecting to install it like so, clicking **Install Playwright**:

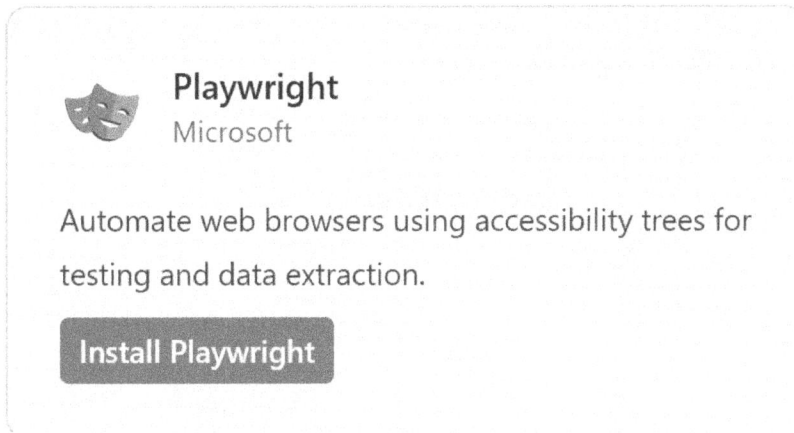

Figure 8.3 – Install Playwright

Now, you should see a dialog opening in your VS Code giving you more information on the server, along with installation instructions. We had previously located the installation information by going to its GitHub repo, but this is also a great way to do it.

Okay, so it seems the answer is to either manually copy-paste what you need in mcp.json or use one of the many options in VS Code.

Step 2: Managing the server

Now, you've added the server, so your mcp.json looks similar to the following JSON (note how Playwright is added):

```json
{
    "servers": {
        "playwright": {
            "command": "npx",
            "args": [
            "@playwright/mcp@latest"
            ]
        }
    },
    "inputs": []
}
```

It's now time to see how the user interface supports us. One thing we can do is select **Extensions**; we should see our list of installed servers like so:

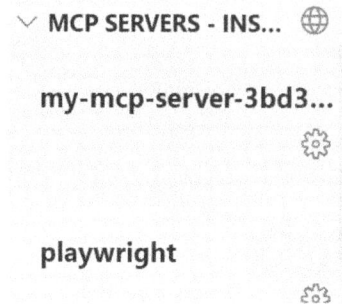

∨ **MCP SERVERS - INS...** ⊕

my-mcp-server-3bd3...

⚙

playwright

⚙

Figure 8.4 – Installed servers

From this view, we can click the cog wheel on a server to interact with it:

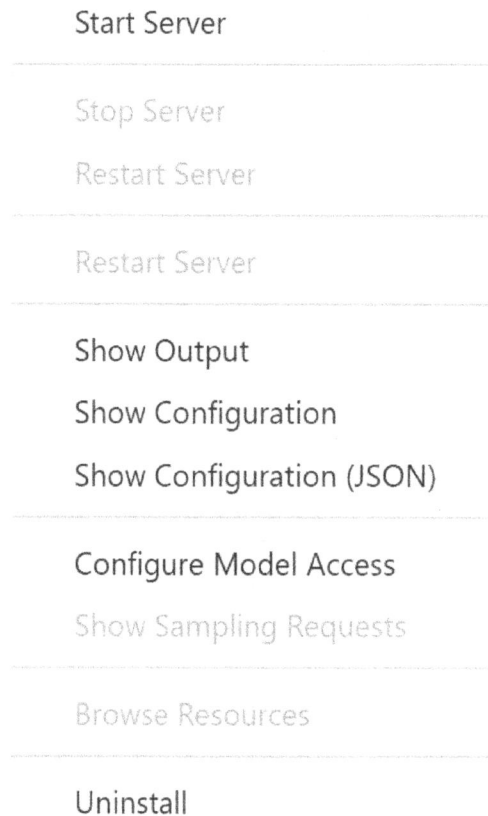

Start Server

Stop Server

Restart Server

Restart Server

Show Output

Show Configuration

Show Configuration (JSON)

Configure Model Access

Show Sampling Requests

Browse Resources

Uninstall

Figure 8.5 – Interacting with the server

As you can see, there are multiple options, from starting the server to seeing its logs, and even JSON configuration. You can take these actions from within the mcp.json file as well.

Step 3: Interacting with the server

Let's start the server, and now let's turn to the chat interface we have from installing GitHub Copilot. Make sure the agent is selected in the droplist and then type the following prompt:

```
Navigate to https://tfl.gov.uk/. I want to go from Paddington to Heathrow,
show me how to get there by underground, important use playwright tool
```

> 💡 Sometimes, VS Code is a bit unwilling to use a tool, so it's worth spending some time on the prompt to ensure it does use it. I've added important use playwright tool to ensure the tool is triggered.

You should see the following in the chat interface:

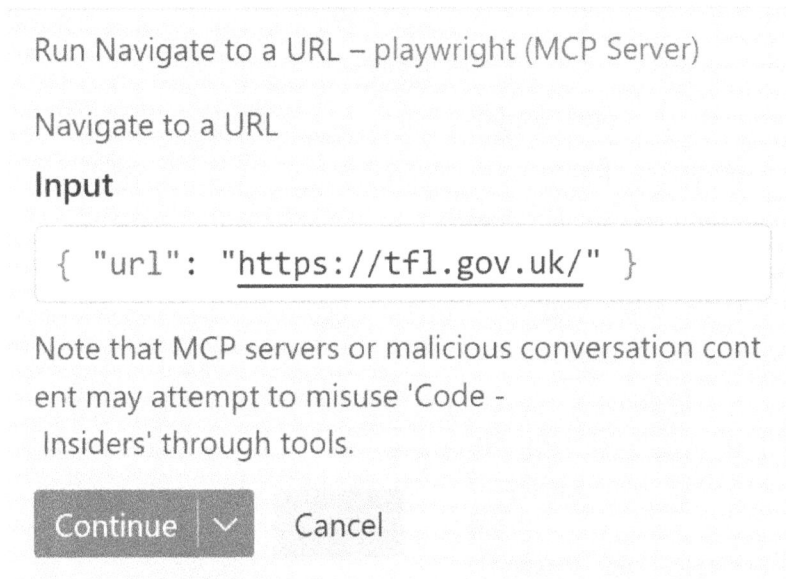

Run Navigate to a URL – playwright (MCP Server)

Navigate to a URL

Input

{ "url": "https://tfl.gov.uk/" }

Note that MCP servers or malicious conversation cont ent may attempt to misuse 'Code - Insiders' through tools.

Continue ∨   Cancel

Figure 8.6 – Using the tool

This shows a tool being triggered, and you being asked to allow the tool to run as part of this. You can see how the URL is parsed out from your prompt and matched as the input to the Playwright tool. This should trigger a whole series of tool calls as Playwright will go through the website, locate the input field, and try to complete the mission set out by the prompt.

You might need to restart the chat sometimes, but once it works as it should, you should see something like the following figure, indicating that Playwright has started to navigate the site properly and is trying to get you from Paddington to Heathrow:

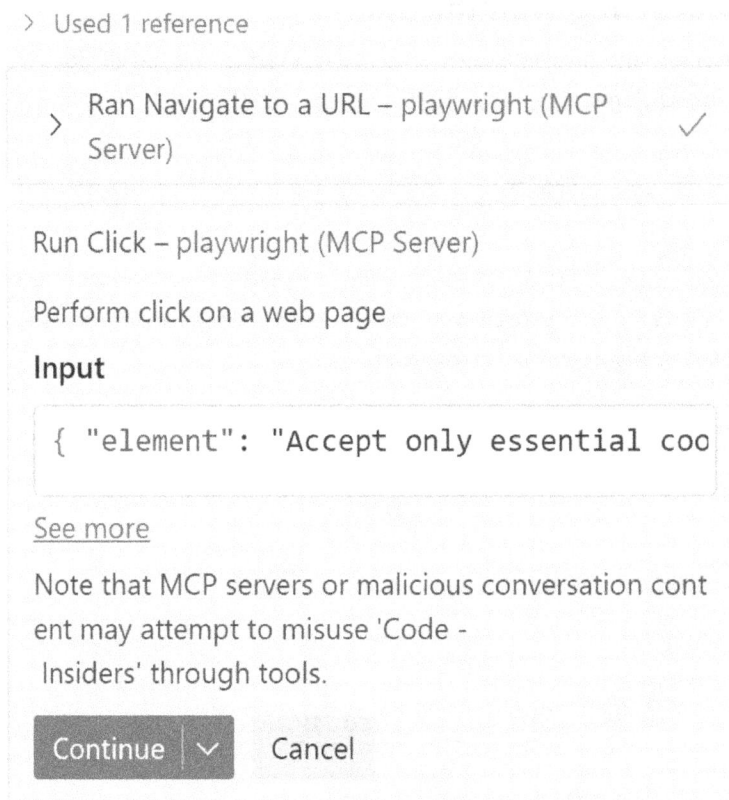

> Used 1 reference

> Ran Navigate to a URL – playwright (MCP Server)   ✓

Run Click – playwright (MCP Server)

Perform click on a web page

Input

{ "element": "Accept only essential coo

See more

Note that MCP servers or malicious conversation content may attempt to misuse 'Code - Insiders' through tools.

Continue ∨   Cancel

Figure 8.7 – Playwright query

Once it's done, you can interact with it in various ways to get what you need and even ask it to generate the Playwright tests from this interaction, which is where the real value lies.

Local and global install

So far, we've installed servers in `.vscode/mcp.json`, which means they are installed into this workspace only. You can install servers globally on your machine as well. To choose that instead, let's use `MCP: Add Server` from the command palette. At the last step, choose **Global**, and it will create an `mcp.json` file in `(Settings)/User/mcp/json`, which means it has added the server entry to the user setting rather than this specific workspace instance. That means that if you open up another instance of VS Code, you will not need to install this server again.

Here's what the user-level `mcp.json` file looks like after a server has been globally installed:

```json
{
    "servers": {
        "my-mcp-server-6801ea17": {
            "url": "https://learn.microsoft.com/api/mcp",
            "type": "http"
        }
    },
    "inputs": []
}
```

As you can see, there's no difference in how it's installed in the actual `mcp.json` file, but the difference is in where the `mcp.json` file is located. The general rule of thumb is, if it's a server you use often, install it globally; if not, install it in the workspace at `.vscode/mcp.json`.

Tips and tricks

So far, we've gone through the basics, but what else is there to know? Well, there are quite a few different settings. A complete listing of features can be found at this docs page: `https://code.visualstudio.com/docs/copilot/chat/mcp-servers`.

Debugging

As a developer, knowing how to debug is a critical skill, so let's show how to do that. Currently, Node.js debugging is supported, according to the documentation (`https://code.visualstudio.com/docs/copilot/customization/mcp-servers#_debug-an-mcp-server`):

```json
"server-ts": {
    "command": "node",
    "args": ["08 - consuming servers/code/build/index.js"],
    "dev": {
        "watch": "08 - consuming servers/code/build/**/*.js",
        "debug": { "type": "node" }
    }
}
```

According to the preceding configuration, what you need to do is this:

1.   Set up your `command` and `args` properties to instruct how to run the server.

2.   Add dev with two different attributes: `watch`, which is a **global pattern (GLOB)** that looks at your JavaScript files for changes, and debug, which is where you specify which process is debugging it. In this case, it's Node. Once it's set up and the server is running, there should be a gray **debug** text just above. Make sure you've added a breakpoint in suitable places, such as starting the server, running a tool, and so on. Here's how you can test different scenarios:

  1.   **Testing startup**: Here, we've just added a breakpoint to our startup code, and all we need to do is start the server from `mcp.json`. You should see how the breakpoint is hit, like so:

```
10   server.registerTool("add", {
11       title: "Addition Tool",
12       description: "Add two numbers",
13       inputSchema: { a: z.number(), b: z.number() }
14   }, async ({ a, b }) => ({
15       content: [{ type: "text", text: String(a + b) }]
16   }));
17   // Start receiving messages on stdin and sending messages on stdout
18   async function main() {
19       console. log("Starting MCP server...");
20       const transport = new StdioServerTransport();
21       await server.connect(transport);
22   }
23   main();
24
```

Figure 8.8 – Breakpoint startup

🔍 **Quick tip:** Need to see a high-resolution version of this image? Open this book in the next-gen Packt Reader or view it in the PDF/ePub copy.

📖 **The next-gen Packt Reader** and a **free PDF/ePub copy** of this book are included with your purchase. Scan the QR code OR visit `https://packtpub.com/unlock`, then use the search bar to find this book by name. Double-check the edition shown to make sure you get the right one.

2. **Testing tools:** A good way to test the tools is to run the inspector in CLI mode. Here's a command for testing a tool, add, with input parameters, a and b. Adopt this command to match the operations and parameters on your server:

```
npx @modelcontextprotocol/inspector --cli node ./build/index.
js --method tools/call --tool-name add --tool-arg a=1 --tool-
arg b=2
```

You should see a response directly in the terminal that looks similar to the following:

```
{
    "content": [
        {
        "type": "text",
        "text": "3"
        }
    ]
}
```

Troubleshooting

Sometimes, you will see an error indication on the *tools* icon in the chat area. If that happens, open the **Output** section in your terminal area, and you will see what the problem is. This area is a good place to inspect generally, as you will see every interaction between VS Code and your server, such as when it starts up and stops servers, but also when it initializes, lists tools, and more.

When we ran the debugger and it connected to the server, we got all this information written to **Output**:

```
2025-08-03 19:18:56.856 [info] Connection state: Starting
2025-08-03 19:18:56.857 [info] Connection state: Running
2025-08-03 19:18:56.857 [info] [editor -> server] {"jsonrpc":"2.0
","id":1,"method":"initialize","params":{"protocolVersion":"2025-
06-18","capabilities":{"roots":{"listChanged":true},"sampli
ng":{},"elicitation":{}},"clientInfo":{"name":"Visual Studio Code -
Insiders","version":"1.103.0-insider"}}}
2025-08-03 19:18:56.888 [warning] [server stderr] Debugger listening on
ws://127.0.0.1:9230/7b07fce3-e6cc-46c7-a0b8-7b782fbe853a
2025-08-03 19:18:56.888 [warning] [server stderr] For help, see: https://
nodejs.org/en/docs/inspector
2025-08-03 19:18:57.052 [warning] [server stderr] Debugger attached.
2025-08-03 19:19:01.960 [info] Waiting for server to respond to
`initialize` request...
2025-08-03 19:19:06.960 [info] Waiting for server to respond to
`initialize` request...
2025-08-03 19:19:10.858 [warning] Failed to parse message: "Starting MCP
server...\n"
2025-08-03 19:19:10.874 [info] [server -> editor]
{"result":{"protocolVersion":"2025-06-18","capabilities":{"tools":{"listC
hanged":true}},"serverInfo":{"name":"demo-server","version":"1.0.0"}},"j-
sonrpc":"2.0","id":1}
2025-08-03 19:19:10.874 [info] [editor -> server]
{"method":"notifications/initialized","jsonrpc":"2.0"}
2025-08-03 19:19:10.874 [info] [editor -> server]
{"jsonrpc":"2.0","id":2,"method":"tools/list","params":{}}
2025-08-03 19:19:10.891 [info] [server -> editor]
{"result":{"tools":[{"name":"add","title":"Addition
Tool","description":"Add two
numbers","inputSchema":{"type":"object","properties":{"a":{"type":"number"},
```

```
"b":{"type":"number"}},"required":["a","b"],"additionalProperties":false,
"$schema":"http://json-schema.org/draft-07/
schema#"}}]},"jsonrpc":"2.0","id":2}
2025-08-03 19:19:10.891 [info] Discovered 1 tools
2025-08-03 19:26:34.115 [warning] [server stderr] Debugger ending on
ws://127.0.0.1:9230/7b07fce3-e6cc-46c7-a0b8-7b782fbe853a
2025-08-03 19:26:34.115 [warning] [server stderr] For help, see: https://
nodejs.org/en/docs/inspector
```

Let's highlight some interesting parts from the preceding response:

- **Editor handshakes with server**: Here, the editor sends information to the server on what features/capabilities it supports. It says to the server that it supports roots, sampling, and elicitation:

```
2025-08-03 19:18:56.857 [info] [editor -> server] {"jsonrpc":"2.0",
"id":1,"method":"initialize","params":{"protocolVersion":"2025-06-18",
"capabilities":{"roots":{"listChanged":true},"sampling":{},
"elicitation":{}},"clientInfo":{"name":"Visual Studio Code -
Insiders"
,"version":"1.103.0-insider"}}}
```

- **Server responds to editor handshake**: Here, the response comes back to say that tools are supported:

```
2025-08-03 19:19:10.874 [info] [server -> editor] {"result":
{"protocolVersion":"2025-06-18","capabilities":{"tools":{"listChang
ed"
:true}},"serverInfo":{"name":"demo-server","version":"1.0.0"}},"json
rpc":"2.0","id":1}
```

- **Server sends initialized notification**: The last step in the handshake is sending the initialized notification. This is something the client sends to the server to say it's ready to exchange data. In this case, our client is VS Code:

```
2025-08-03 19:19:10.874 [info] [editor -> server]
{"method":"notifications/initialized","jsonrpc":"2.0"}
```

- **Tell me about your tools**: Now the client asks the server for its tools:

```
2025-08-03 19:19:10.874 [info] [editor -> server]
{"jsonrpc":"2.0","id":2,"method":"tools/list","params":{}}
```

- **Server responds to tools request**: Lastly, the server responds to a request to list its tools with the following:

```
2025-08-03 19:19:10.891 [info] [server -> editor] {"result":{"tools"
:[{"name":"add","title":"Addition Tool","description":"Add two
numbers"
,"inputSchema":{"type":"object","properties":{"a":{"type":
"number"},"b":{"type":"number"}},"required":["a","b"],"additional
Properties":false,"$schema":"http://json-schema.org/draft-07/schema#
"}}]},"jsonrpc":"2.0","id":2}
```

Tool management

Tool management is an important aspect of using VS Code. There are some interesting scenarios around tools where your editor helps:

- **Selecting and deselecting tools**: When you add servers, it might add a lot of tools at once. For both scenarios, where you use your editor as an agentic tool and also where you want to ensure the correct tool is called, you can choose which tools are active. You can make this selection by clicking the *tools* icon in the chat, which will bring up a user interface of all tools. Select/deselect the tools you want to have active or inactivate.

- **Run a specific tool**: Generally, when you want to run tools, you try to type a prompt that matches a specific tool's description as much as possible. If you want to make sure that the correct tool is chosen, you can prefix it with #, which will identify that specific tool. For example, to run a tool called add, you can craft a prompt like so:

```
#add 2 and 7
```

- **Managing the number of tools**: Some models have limitations on how many tools they can accept. To address this, there's a setting called github.copilot.chat.virtualTools. enabled, which will analyze the prompt and only submit the tools that match the prompt. This is a great way to avoid any errors as a result of using too many prompts. Make sure you're on the latest version of VS Code Insider. This feature is in active development and may change over time.

- **Handle tool approval**: When VS Code decides it wants to run a tool, it displays it as a query asking you to click **Continue**. At this point, you can choose to allow it only for this prompt session, for this workspace, or to always allow. Here's how it works:

1. Type the following prompt:

    ```
    #add 2 and 7
    ```

    This makes VS Code ask you to click **Continue**. Now, select from the dropdown to allow for this workspace. Let's run it again.

2. Type the following prompt:

    ```
    #add 2 and 9
    ```

    This ran the tool without asking for my consent, as I had previously given it permission to run in this workspace. To undo this consent, I can run Chat: Reset Tool Confirmations from the command palette.

Other settings

There are a lot of settings being added all the time to both Copilot and VS Code. Make sure you're in VS Code Insiders, type MCP in the command palette, and you will see many dedicated MCP settings:

> mcp
MCP: Reset Cached Tools   recently used ⚙
MCP: Reset Trust
MCP: Open User Configuration
MCP: Add Server...
Accounts: Manage Trusted **MCP** Servers For Account   other commands
Extensions: Focus on **MCP** Servers - Installed View
Markdown: Change Preview Security Settings
MCP: Browse Resources...
MCP: Browse Servers
MCP: List Servers
MCP: Open Remote User Configuration
MCP: Open Workspace Folder MCP Configuration
MCP: Show Installed Servers

Figure 8.9 – MCP commands

As you can see, there are quite a lot of commands available. Try typing Copilot as well, as it's used in conjunction with MCP. This is a changing area, though, but if you are developing MCP servers, it's part of your job to leverage your editor to the best of your ability.

Security aspects

Security is a huge topic, but let's discuss it in the context of using an editor. There are things you can do generally to stay safer, so let's try to summarize a good list of practices:

- **Keep secrets out of configuration**: Here's how you can do that by specifying the configuration in the mcp.json file:

```
{
  "mcp": {
    "inputs": [
      {
        "type": "promptString",
        "id": "my-key",
        "description": "Token for my API",
        "password": true
      }
    ],
    "servers": {
      "my-server": {
        "type": "http",
        "url": "https://my-secure-api/mcp",
        "headers" : {
          "Authorization": "Bearer ${input:my-key}"
        }
      }
    }
  }
}
```

By using the inputs element, you can ensure that secrets are kept out of the configuration file. How it works is that when the server is started, the user interface will prompt you to fill in the value for my-key, and it will be stored securely. The value can then be referenced in the server entry by using ${input:my-key}. For every request to https://my-secure-api/mcp, the Authorization header will be added with the value you provided.

- **Tool running access**: It's recommended to disallow continuous access for a tool running in a workspace. Prefer giving it access each time it's asked for. It also gives you the chance to check the parsed input.

- **Restrict what a server can do:** There are ways to restrict what a server can access. For example, there's an MCP server for file access. You should restrict it to one folder at most or folders where you're sure it can't do any harm.

- **Use trusted servers:** GitHub recently released a registry of vetted MCP servers. Using the latest version of VS Code Insiders, you can type @mcp, and it will show a list of MCP servers that you can install. You can access that same list by choosing the MCP: Add Server command and then selecting **Browse MCP Servers**. Your list of servers should look similar to this figure:

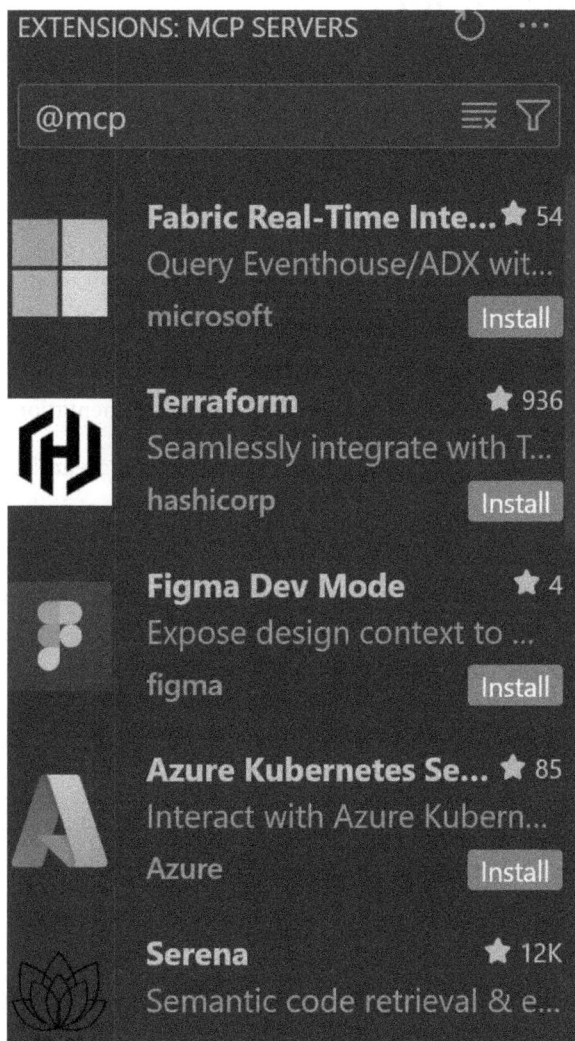

Figure 8.10 – MCP registry

In general, make sure the author behind a server is a reputable source (e.g., Stripe is behind the Stripe MCP server, and so on). Even then, resort to code scanning tools and keep track of the latest security news; breaches happen all the time. The same registry can also be found via this link (`https://code.visualstudio.com/insider/mcp`), but I prefer using the built-in experience in VS Code. Also, check out the GitHub repo for servers, as that allows you to read more on each server via their README files (`https://github.com/modelcontextprotocol/servers`).

Suggestion for servers

So what servers are recommended? Well, it depends on your needs, but I would personally use the following:

- **GitHub** (`https://github.com/github/github-mcp-server`): This server makes my life a lot easier as I can interact with issues, **pull requests (PRs)**, delegate work to agents, and more
- **Playwright** (`https://github.com/microsoft/playwright-mcp`): This is great for navigating sites, but also generates tests from that navigation, thereby saving a lot of time
- **Microsoft Learn MCP server** (`https://github.com/microsoftdocs/mcp`): This is the official Microsoft Docs and Learn server, which provides documentation directly in your editor

There are many more, but start with these and see what fits your scenario.

Summary

In this chapter, we went through how to consume an MCP server, both the ones you create and external ones. Additionally, we discussed how to manage servers once installed, their configuration, tool usage, and more.

Finally, we provided some tips on security practices. This should be seen as a bare minimum set of practices, and you should do more.

In the next chapter, we'll cover sampling, an advanced topic but very useful when the server needs to delegate work to you as the user.

Assignment

Install a server of your choice, and try it out via a prompt. Try installing a server from here: `https://code.visualstudio.com/insider/mcp`.

Quiz

How do you install an MCP server?

- A: You can install it in the same way you install extensions in VS Code.
- B: You run `mcp install <server name>` in the terminal.
- C: Servers are installed by adding text entries to `mcp.json`. You also need to specify how to start it or where the server resides.

You can access the solution at `https://github.com/PacktPublishing/Learn-Model-Context-Protocol-with-Python/blob/main/Chapter08/solutions/solution-quiz.md`.

Unlock this book's exclusive benefits now   UNLOCK NOW

Scan this QR code or go to `https://packtpub.com/unlock`, then search this book by name.

Note: Keep your purchase invoice ready before you start.

9

Sampling

One of the most powerful features of MCP is **sampling**. What does that mean, first of all? Well, let's take a look at the definition of the word and deduce from there. Merriam-Webster defines sampling as follows:

> *"the action or process of taking samples of something for analysis"*

Okay, so we need a sample, and we end up analyzing said sample, understood. With this definition in mind, let's talk about it in the context of MCP. In MCP, sampling means the server is sending a sampling request, a *sample* for analysis, to the client. Why does the server do that? It's simple; the server needs the client's help with some things. Because the client is the one with the LLM (even though a server can have an LLM sometimes), the server delegates tasks to the client, where an LLM can help.

Makes sense so far, right? But I bet you're asking why a server would do that.

In this chapter, we'll do the following:

- Understand the topic of sampling and when to use it
- Build a server implementation using sampling and consume it with VS Code
- Connect the server implementation to a client implementation for the occasions when we want to integrate this functionality into our app.

The chapter covers the following topics:

- Why sampling?
- Implementing sampling

Why sampling?

As we said at the beginning, the server wants to delegate some problems to the client and, specifically, to the client's LLM. So, what problems can an LLM help with that the server can't? There are lots of examples if you think about it: generating product descriptions, abstracts, tags, and more.

Let's look into the sample flow first so we understand how the interaction happens at a high level.

Sampling flow

When performing sampling, the following participants are involved:

- **User**: The user is usually involved in two places, as the originator of the initial action, and even as the *human in the loop*, accepting or modifying the sample request.
- **Server**: The server is the participant sending out a sample request. This request is usually sent out from a server feature, such as a tool call, reading of a resource, or a request from a prompt template.
- **Client**: The client's job is to receive the sample request and show it to the user, so the user can decide what to do with it. A user treats a sampling request as a recommendation for what to do. If the request asks for a specific model, number of tokens, and so on, then this is something the user can take under advisement, and either accept or change to their liking.
- **LLM**: The LLM on the client plays the part of completing the sampling request and takes a prompt originating from the server, and produces a response using its generative capabilities.

Here's a diagram depicting the overall flow:

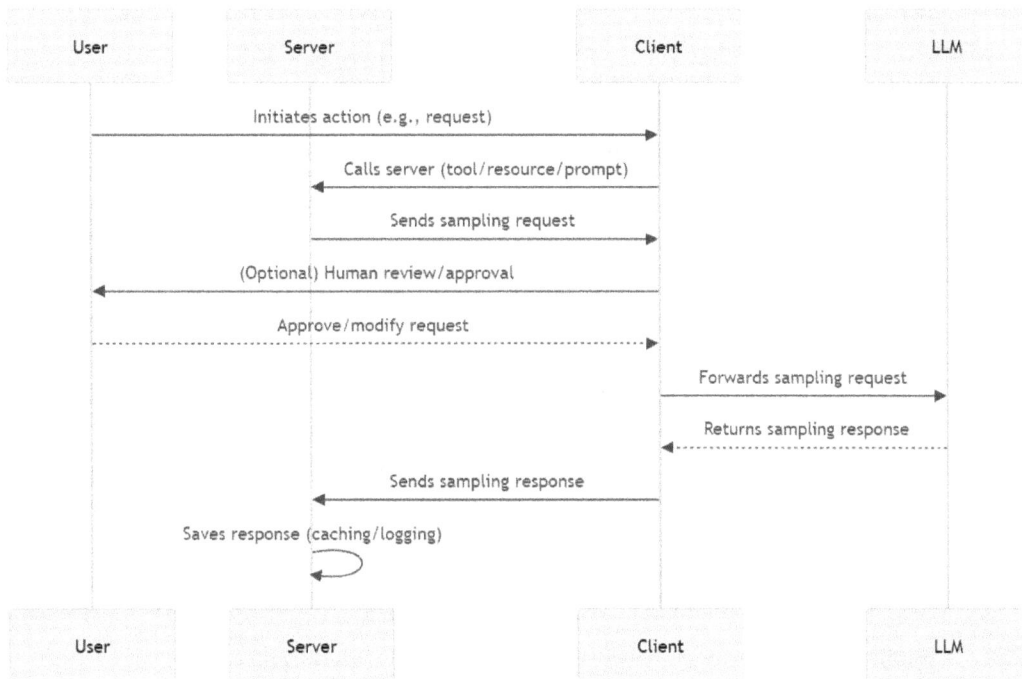

Figure 9.1 – Sampling flow

🔍 **Quick tip:** Need to see a high-resolution version of this image? Open this book in the next-gen Packt Reader or view it in the PDF/ePub copy.

📖 **The next-gen Packt Reader** and a **free PDF/ePub copy** of this book are included with your purchase. Scan the QR code OR visit https://packtpub.com/unlock, then use the search bar to find this book by name. Double-check the edition shown to make sure you get the right one.

It's worth clarifying that a sampling request doesn't happen for no reason, but rather, there's an initial action that ends up triggering it. For example, the user wants to create a product, or needs help with a blog post, and so on, and that in turn leads to the server delegating part of that task back to the client.

Let's look at some specific scenarios next to understand it better.

Scenarios

We've mentioned some scenarios briefly up to this point, but let's discuss them in detail.

Writing a blog post

The act of writing a blog post is a good case, as there are aspects of it that definitely fall on the user, such as writing a draft. However, there are parts of it when an LLM does a better job, such as summarizing it for an abstract or even generating keywords (thank you, Kent Dodds, for the inspiration for this use case):

1. The user submits a draft blog post to the server.
2. The server stores the draft but asks for help with producing tags, so a sample request is sent.
3. The client uses its LLM to analyze the draft and produce a response.

Back office e-commerce

A common task for someone working in a back office as part of e-commerce is the management of products. Usually, you start off registering the product by title and capture other properties that might make sense. However, writing a compelling description might be a time-consuming task and something an LLM does better than a human. Here's how this use case could look as a sampling scenario:

1. The admin user, via the client, adds a new product with a title and keywords.
2. The server asks the client for help with creating a compelling product description with keywords as context.
3. The client produces such a description, and the server updates the product with a better description.

Mystery game

Many times, when playing games, you encounter characters in the game you want to have a conversation with; some of these characters are known as **NPCs** or **non-player characters**. Usually, these characters are limited in what they can say, as this is how they're programmed. This limitation takes away from the gaming experience, and this is where an LLM can step in and do a better job. See the following flow for how this could work:

1. The user asks to talk to a character.
2. The server retrieves character information such as name, description, motive, clues, and so on, and sends it as a sample request.
3. The client retrieves the character information from the prompt request and uses that as a system message to produce a nice conversation response.

Now that we understand more about suitable scenarios, let's discuss what the actual messages look like, as it's important to understand what is being sent back and forth. More importantly, it's important to understand what information you can configure upon sending a sample request to a client.

Messages

If you're using an SDK, you will almost never encounter a JSON-RPC, but what is interesting to know is what can be sent as part of a sampling request, so you know what type of guidance you can send to the client. Let's have a look at the following message:

Request

```
{
  "jsonrpc": "2.0",
  "id": 1,
  "method": "sampling/createMessage",
  "params": {
    "messages": [
      {
        "role": "user",
        "content": {
```

```
            "type": "text",
            "text": "Write a compelling description of this product:
               tomato, here's some keywords: red, vegetable, fresh"
          }
        }
      ],
      "modelPreferences": {
        "hints": [
          {
            "name": "claude-3-sonnet"
          }
        ],
        "intelligencePriority": 0.8,
        "speedPriority": 0.5
      },
      "systemPrompt": "You're a professional writing assistant and
         tend to want to write descriptions in a poetic way",
      "maxTokens": 100
    }
  }
```

In the preceding message, the following are of special interest:

- messages: Here's where you're sending the messages that get fed to the LLM.
- modelPreferences: This property is just a *preference* for which model should ideally be used. The user is the one ultimately deciding, but this should be seen as a recommendation. Also, make note of other properties we can set, such as intelligencePriority and speedPriority.
- systemPrompt: This is an important one, as this is the *personality* of the LLM and can greatly affect the outcome of the message.
- maxTokens: This property decides how many tokens will be used for this task.

Now that we have had a good look at what the server is sending to the client, let's look at what the client sends back:

Response

```
{
  "jsonrpc": "2.0",
```

```
    "id": 1,
    "result": {
      "role": "assistant",
      "content": {
        "type": "text",
        "text": "The capital of France is Paris."
      },
      "model": "claude-3-sonnet-20240307",
      "stopReason": "endTurn"
    }
}
```

Here, we can see how the LLM response comes back in the content property, and it also lets us know which model was ultimately used, among other details.

Implementing sampling

Now, we've come to the extra exciting part of this chapter, namely, how to implement sampling.

We'll cover the following parts of the implementation:

- **Server side**: How to add this to the MCP server
- **Client side**: How to enable it and what the code looks like, both to receive a request and send a response

Server implementation

To implement sampling on the server side, we need to consider when the sampling request should take place. Usually, a sampling request doesn't happen out of nowhere, but it happens in the context of an action. Imagine the following scenario. A user working in the back office of an e-commerce site adds new products for sale. They need help with the description, and it should be as compelling as possible. For the description, they will therefore use the help of a client and its LLM. Here's how it will play out:

1. The user's client calls a tool on the server that asks to create a new product.
2. The server's tool then dispatches a sample request with instructions on what to do, which is a prompt.

3. The client then takes said prompt from the sample request, calls their LLM, and returns the answer:

```python
from mcp.server.fastmcp import Context, FastMCP
from mcp.server.session import ServerSession
from mcp.types import SamplingMessage, TextContent

from uuid import uuid4

mcp = FastMCP(name="Sampling Example")

products = []

@mcp.tool()
async def create_product(product_name: str, keywords: str,
    ctx: Context[ServerSession, None]) -> str:
    """Create a product and generate a product
        description using LLM sampling."""

    # 1. A new product is being created

    product = { "id": uuid4(), "name": product_name, "description":
        "" }

    prompt = f"Create a product description about {keywords}"

    # 2. Creates a sampling message and passes the prompt as the
    payload

    result = await ctx.session.create_message(
        messages=[
            SamplingMessage(
                role="user",
                content=TextContent(type="text", text=prompt),
            )
        ],
        max_tokens=100,
```

```
        )


        product["description"] = result.content.text


        products.append(product)


        # return the complete product
        return product
```

In steps 1 and 2 in the preceding code, note the use of the ctx (context) object, calling session.create_message, and passing in SamplingMessage, which has a user value, and messages being populated with the prompt you're sending to the client:

```
result = await ctx.session.create_message(
    messages=[
        SamplingMessage(
            role="user",
            content=TextContent(type="text", text=prompt),
        )
    ],
    max_tokens=100,
)

if __name__ == "__main__":
    print("Starting server…")
    mcp.run()
```

Also, take note of the fact that we're waiting for the client here to come back to us before we return. Once the client's message comes back, we assign the result to the product description and, finally, return the product:

```
product["description"] = result.content.text


products.append(product)


# return the complete product
return product
```

Let's test this out in VS Code. Ensure you do the following:

1. Create a server entry in `mcp.json` like so:

    ```
    "sample-server": {
        "command": "python",
        "args": ["path/to/server/sample-server.py"]
    }
    ```

    Make sure the server is running by clicking the **Start Server** link at the top of the server entry.

2. You also need to select which models are allowed to be used with sampling. To make the selection, open the **Extension** view and notice the **MCP Servers – installed** section at the bottom. Click the gear icon and **Configure Model Access** for the installed server, and select the allowed models for sampling, such as **Claude Sonnet**.

3. Open the **GitHub Copilot Chat** window in VS Code and ensure the **Agent** mode is selected in the chat (select the icon for it at the top or run the **Chat: Open Chat** command in the command palette). Now, type the following prompt:

    ```
    "create product called tomato with keywords red and vegetable and
    delicious"
    ```

You should see a dialog asking for your permission to run that, once allowed, produces a tooling response from `create_product`. Here's what happened under the hood:

1. The prompt was parsed. Here's what was sent to the tool:

    ```
    {
        "keywords": "red, vegetable, delicious",
        "product_name": "tomato"
    }
    ```

2. The `create_product` tool was invoked.

3. The sample request was sent to the client. Because the client in VS Code has its own LLM, it produces a response to the sample request like so:

CHAT $+$ ↺ ⚙ ⋯ | ⌈⌉ ✕

create a product tomato with keywords
red, juicy

> Used 1 reference

> Thought for a few seconds

⌄ Ran `create_product` –
   sampling (MCP Server)   ✓

Input

```
{
  "product_name": "tomato",
  "keywords": "red, juicy"
}
```

Output

```
{"id": 1, "name":
"tomato", "description":
"# Garden-Fresh
Tomatoes\n\nPerfectly
**red** and incredibly
**juicy**, our premium
tomatoes are the ideal
addition to your kitchen.
Harvested at peak
ripeness, each tomato
delivers an explosion of
garden-fresh flavor with
every bite.\n\n##
```

📎 Add Context...   {} *mcp.json* $+$

Add context (#), extensions (@), commands

Agent ⌄   Copilot-SWE ⌄   ✂ ☁ ▷⌄

Figure 9.2 – Sampling in VS Code

Let's have a look at the generated description:

```
Introducing our **Red Garden Medley**—a vibrant selection of the freshest,
most delicious red vegetables nature has to offer! Each hand-picked
assortment features juicy tomatoes, crisp red bell peppers, and sweet red
radishes, bursting with flavor and color. Perfect for salads, roasting, or
snacking, these vegetables not only brighten your plate but also deliver a
powerhouse of vitamins and antioxidants. Enjoy the taste of freshness with
every bite—delicious, nutritious, and naturally red!
```

Wouldn't you buy that tomato? :)

Okay, that's great. We got sampling to work on an MCP server, and VS Code was acting as a client, ensuring that it worked. How do we actually build a client for this in a scenario where we want to integrate this into a real solution? That's a great question and something we will cover in the next section.

Client implementation

First off, you need to let the server know that you support sampling as a feature. To do that, you need to pass the configuration when creating the client instance, like so:

```
{
  "capabilities": {
    "sampling": {}
  }
}
```

Okay, what do we need to know? For one, sampling is outside of your normal flow of calling tools, resources, and prompts. What does that mean, you wonder. Well, let's see how we listen for incoming sampling requests:

```
async def run():
    async with stdio_client(server_params) as (read, write):
        async with ClientSession(read, write,
            sampling_callback=handle_sampling_message) as session:

            await session.initialize()

            # call tools, resource and prompts and read responses
```

This code shows how we normally connect to an MCP server and initialize the process so we can later call tools or whatever we want to do. There's a difference, though: note `sampling_callback=handle_sampling_message`. This is important as this allows us to listen for incoming messages.

Let's look at `handle_sampling_message` next:

```python
async def call_llm(prompt: str, system_prompt: str) -> str:
    client = OpenAI(
    base_url="https://models.github.ai/inference",
    api_key=os.environ["GITHUB_TOKEN"],
)

    response = client.chat.completions.create(
        messages=[
            {
                "role": "system",
                "content": system_prompt,
            },
            {
                "role": "user",
                "content": prompt,
            }
        ],
        model="openai/gpt-4o-mini",
        temperature=1,
        max_tokens=200,
        top_p=1
    )

    return response.choices[0].message.content

async def handle_sampling_message(
    context: RequestContext[ClientSession, None], params:
        types.CreateMessageRequestParams
) -> types.CreateMessageResult:
    print(f"Sampling request: {params.messages}")
```

```python
# 1. parse out the incoming prompt
message = params.messages[0].content.text

# 2. call the llm to get a response on our prompt query
response = await call_llm(message, "You're a helpful assistant,
    keep to the topic, don't make things up too much but
        definitely create a compelling product description")

# 3. create the sample response
return types.CreateMessageResult(
    role="assistant",
    content=types.TextContent(
        type="text",
        text=response,
    ),
    model="gpt-3.5-turbo",
    stopReason="endTurn",
)
```

There are three things in the preceding code we should make a note of:

- In step 1, here's how we parse out the incoming product message (our assignment, if you will). This is what we will send to the LLM to get a response from. In this case, our response should be a product description.
- In step 2, we call the LLM to get a response.
- Lastly, we construct a sample response that gets sent back to the MCP server.

A helper function calls GitHub Models with a prompt and a system message, and parses out the LLM response.

That's it, if you test running the client at this point: https://github.com/PacktPublishing/Learn-Model-Context-Protocol-with-Python/blob/main/Chapter09/code/python/README.md

You should see a response similar to the following:

```
[08/16/25 19:31:40] INFO        Processing request of type CallToolRequest
server.py:624
Sampling request: [SamplingMessage(role='user',
content=TextContent(type='text', text='Create a product description
about paprika described by as red, juicy, vegetable', annotations=None,
```

meta=None))]

[08/16/25 19:31:43] INFO   Processing request of type ListToolsRequest
server.py:624
result: {"id": 1, "name": "paprika", "description": "**Product
Description: Paprika \u2013 The Vibrant Touch of Flavor**\n\nElevate your
culinary creations with our premium Paprika, a stunning red spice derived
from the most luscious, juicy peppers. This vibrant addition is more than
just a seasoning; it\u2019s a burst of color and taste that brings warmth
and depth to every dish.\n\nOur Paprika is sourced from high-quality, sun-
ripened vegetables, meticulously harvested at their peak to ensure maximum
flavor. With its rich, sweet notes and subtle smokiness, this natural
spice delivers a delightful punch that enhances everything from savory
stews and roasted meats to vibrant vegetable dishes and sauces.\n\nNot
only is our Paprika a feast for the eyes with its brilliant red hue, but
it's also packed with antioxidants and vitamins, making it a nutritious
choice for health-conscious cooks. Whether you sprinkle it onto a beloved
family recipe or use it to create something intentionally new, our Paprika
is versatile enough to brighten any meal.\n\nTransform everyday cooking
into an extraordinary experience with the irresistible"}
                        INFO   Processing request of type CallToolRequest
server.py:624

result: {
  "id": 1,
  "name": "paprika",
  "description": "**Product Description: Paprika – The Vibrant Touch of
Flavor**\n\nElevate your culinary creations with our premium Paprika, a
stunning red spice derived from the most luscious, juicy peppers. This
vibrant addition is more than just a seasoning; it's a burst of color
and taste that brings warmth and depth to every dish.\n\nOur Paprika is
sourced from high-quality, sun-ripened vegetables, meticulously harvested
at their peak to ensure maximum flavor. With its rich, sweet notes and
subtle smokiness, this natural spice delivers a delightful punch that
enhances everything from savory stews and roasted meats to vibrant
vegetable dishes and sauces.\n\nNot only is our Paprika a feast for the
eyes with its brilliant red hue, but it's also packed with antioxidants
and vitamins, making it a nutritious choice for health-conscious cooks.
Whether you sprinkle it onto a beloved family recipe or use it to create
something intentionally new, our Paprika is versatile enough to brighten
any meal.\n\nTransform everyday cooking into an extraordinary experience

```
with the irresistible"
}
```

The client does two things:

- It calls the create_product tool with a product name and keyword, and it ends up producing a product with an LLM-generated description like so:

```
Product Description: Paprika – The Vibrant Touch of Flavor**\n\
nElevate your culinary creations with our premium Paprika, a
stunning red spice derived from the most luscious, juicy peppers.
This vibrant addition is more than just a seasoning; it's a burst
of color and taste that brings warmth and depth to every dish.\n\
nOur Paprika is sourced from high-quality, sun-ripened vegetables,
meticulously harvested at their peak to ensure maximum flavor. With
its rich, sweet notes and subtle smokiness, this natural spice
delivers a delightful punch that enhances everything from savory
stews and roasted meats to vibrant vegetable dishes and sauces.\n\
nNot only is our Paprika a feast for the eyes with its brilliant red
hue, but it's also packed with antioxidants and vitamins, making it
a nutritious choice for health-conscious cooks. Whether you sprinkle
it onto a beloved family recipe or use it to create something
intentionally new, our Paprika is versatile enough to brighten any
meal.\n\nTransform everyday cooking into an extraordinary experience
with the irresistible
```

  Doesn't that sound like paprika you would buy? Imagine sending this to an LLM and asking it to generate a photo (optional homework). What an image that would be.

- It calls the get_products tool, which lists the newly added product.

As you can see, this is a great way to delegate tasks to the client that it's better equipped to handle.

Summary

The idea with the meaning of the word *sampling* is to analyze a small sample. In the context of MCP, this is about delegation and how the server delegates part of its work to the client.

A scenario is usually started by a user, such as authoring a blog post or wanting to create a product in a back office solution. The server ends up creating a sampling request and sends that to the client as part of a task it needs help with. The client is then able to respond to said request using an LLM response.

It should also be stated that the sample request contains recommendations on model, token usage, system prompt, and much more, and that it should involve a human who either accepts these recommendations or changes them to their liking.

This is a great functionality, where an LLM on the client can be called in to help.

In our next chapter, we'll dive into yet another powerful feature of MCP, namely, elicitation, which is about improving the user experience by setting up a flow where the user is asked to pick another choice or provide more information to help the server do its job better.

Assignment

In this assignment, we'll take all our knowledge of adding sampling implementations to the client and server and apply it to a fun area, namely, a mystery game, and the conversational part. The idea is to create a character that's interesting to talk to over pre-programmed responses.

Here's how it should work:

- **User:** Talk to character *N*
- **Server:** Retrieve character info
- **Server:** Send sampling request with character info
- **Client:** Receive sampling request and produce a response using the LLM
- **Server:** Store response for caching and logging

To help you, imagine that a character is defined in a JSON file like so:

```
[
  {
    "id": "1",
    "name": "Monsieur Lestrange",
    "description": "a 600 year old vampire",
    "personality": "very polite and will tell you a great deal of what
      it's like paying the electricity bill of a 1200 year old castle
      with bad insulation. In fact, he's quite boring and would rather
      talk about that over what you would expect like vampire hunters,
      stakes etc"

  }
]
```

Solution

You can access the solution at `https://github.com/PacktPublishing/Learn-Model-Context-Protocol-with-Python/blob/main/Chapter09/solution/README.md`.

Quiz

What's the reason for using sampling?

- A: You want to sample a smaller piece of information from a large dataset
- B: The server needs help with a generative AI-type task, and the client can use its LLM to generate a response
- C: The client needs the server's help with a task

What party initiates the sampling request?

- A: Either of them
- B: The client
- C: The server

You can access the solution at `https://github.com/PacktPublishing/Learn-Model-Context-Protocol-with-Python/blob/main/Chapter09/solution/solution-quiz.md`.

10

Elicitation

Elicitation means the process of getting or producing something, especially information or a reaction.

Why does that matter for MCP then? The official docs have the following to say:

> The **Model Context Protocol (MCP)** *provides a standardized way for servers to request additional information from users through the client during interactions. This flow allows clients to maintain control over user interactions and data sharing while enabling servers to gather necessary information dynamically.*

So, what does that mean? It means, for some reason, the server finds it needs to involve the client additionally to ask the user for more information. Now the purpose is clearer, right?

Okay, imagine the following: as a user, you're trying to book a holiday trip, and the date you searched for isn't available. There's a way to improve that situation through using elicitation – namely, instead of just saying as a server that said trip isn't available, you make an effort to ask additional questions and perhaps suggest dates around this date that are available. Now you'll see, hopefully, how this could be a very useful technique in lots of contexts, to increase the chance of something being sold or booked, and so on.

In this chapter, we'll learn how to do the following:

- Explain what elicitation is
- Learn when to use it
- Build an elicitation integration

The chapter covers the following topics:

- Why elicitation?
- Implementing elicitation
- Elicitation flow
- JSON-RPC messages
- Implementing the server-side functionality
- Testing elicitation with VS Code

Why elicitation?

Okay, we've already tried describing, at the beginning of this chapter, what situations might motivate the use of elicitation in MCP, but let's try to summarize some main motivating factors:

- **Task complexity**: For some tasks, it's simply not possible to provide all the information needed up front. This might be scenarios where the user needs to make selections through a workflow. For example, the user might need to make multiple choices as they purchase a ticket to the movies. They start with wanting to book a certain film on a given day, but then need to be asked whether they need a premium seat or other customizations available. Or, take a scenario such as booking a train ticket, where you need to make choices such as a ticket with a numbered seat, whether the ticket is physical or an e-ticket, and so on. You could ask for all this information up front, but it might make for a tedious user experience, and it might be better to start off asking for less input.

- **Increase the conversion rate on a website**: Another angle is for companies to ensure they have a better *conversion rate*, meaning that more users on the website become actual customers. For example, if a user wants a red sweater and you don't have it in stock at the moment, then you might want to ask the user if they're okay with a different color or want to sign up on a waitlist to order it automatically when it comes in. This type of behavior is more likely to improve your sales as a company.

- **Improved user experience**: As a logical conclusion of the preceding angle, the overall user experience is likely to improve if the user can be met with something else than just a *no*, and instead be faced with reasonable choices.

All in all, elicitation can be a great way to improve your app. Let's try to look at the implementation side of things next.

Implementing elicitation

So, we want to use elicitation – great. But first, there's a set of guidelines we should know about. Here's what the official docs have to say:

For trust, safety, and security:

- Servers *must not* use elicitation to request sensitive information

Applications *should*:

- Provide a UI that makes it clear which server is requesting information
- Allow users to review and modify their responses before sending
- Respect user privacy and provide clear decline and cancel options

Elicitation flow

In general, what happens during elicitation is that the server decides it doesn't have enough information to complete a call to a tool, resource, or prompt.

What's important to understand is that this happens as a two-step process:

1. The server asks the client if it's okay to initiate an elicitation request towards the user.
2. The client asks the user to submit information.

The user can both accept or decline in both 1) and 2); see the following sequence diagram explaining this process. To hopefully make it easier to understand, we've chosen a trip-booking process:

Figure 10.1 – JSON-RPC messages

JSON-RPC messages

Now that we've explained the overall flow, let's see what the JSON-RPC messages look like.

Like with most MCP features, there are specific messages in JSON-RPC that need to be sent and received:

Request message

```json
{
  "jsonrpc": "2.0",
  "id": 1,
  "method": "elicitation/create",
  "params": {
    "message": "Please provide your GitHub username",
    "requestedSchema": {
      "type": "object",
      "properties": {
        "name": {
          "type": "string"
        }
      },
      "required": ["name"]
    }
  }
}
```

In the preceding message, we can see how `message` contains the payload for what we're asking for – a user choice to be made or some explanation of what we're asking for. `requestedSchema` is a schema that defines what information you need as a server, so here it's important you specify both the name of what you need, its type, and any other rules you want to impose. See this example schema, where the server asks for name, email, and age. For each parameter, we specify both type and description, and in some places, we specify format and even validation rules, such as you should be at least 18 years of age:

```json
"requestedSchema": {
    "type": "object",
    "properties": {
      "name": {
        "type": "string",
        "description": "Your full name"
      },
      "email": {
        "type": "string",
```

```
      "format": "email",
      "description": "Your email address"
    },
    "age": {
      "type": "number",
      "minimum": 18,
      "description": "Your age"
    }
  },
  "required": ["name", "email"]
}
```

Let's have a look at a response. Specifically, this is an *accept*-type response where the user has agreed to submit the information requested of them.

Response message

```
{
  "jsonrpc": "2.0",
  "id": 2,
  "result": {
    "action": "accept",
    "content": {
      "name": "Monalisa Octocat",
      "email": "octocat@github.com",
      "age": 30
    }
  }
}
```

It's actually possible for the user to say, *"I don't want to provide this information"*. If that happens, then a reject type message is sent as a response instead, and looks like so:

Reject message

```
{
  "sonrpc": "2.0",
  "id": 2,
  "result": {
```

```
        "action": "decline"
    }
}
```

Here, it's clear that the user declines to submit the requested information.

A third type of response is cancellation. It's very similar to decline, but it's more like the user dismisses the elicitation dialog by typing *Escape*, clicking to close a dialog, so it's more like the user ignores interacting, rather than saying an explicit *No*.

Request schema types

We've mentioned the general request schema and an example. However, there are quite a few supported types, and it's important to know they exist so you use them correctly. These types are presented to the user as part of the elicitation process, and it means the user either uses a drop list, a text input field, or some other UI element to provide the information.

- `string`: This one is about asking for a string. You can add quite a few checks. Here's what the schema looks like:

  ```
  {
      "type": "string",
      "title": "Display Name",
      "description": "Description text",
      "minLength": 3,
      "maxLength": 50,
      "pattern": "^[A-Za-z]+$",
      "format": "email"
  }
  ```

  Here, you can see that you can limit both `minLength` and `maxLength` and even set patterns, which can be highly useful in case you're asking for a specific allowed structure, such as an address, telephone number, social security number, and so on.

- `number`: This one is slightly less complex, but by setting a minimum and maximum value, it helps the user understand what's allowed and not. See this schema:

  ```
  {
      "type": "number", // or "integer"
      "title": "Display Name",
  ```

```
        "description": "Description text",
        "minimum": 0,
        "maximum": 100
    }
```

See the `minimum` and `maximum` values, which you can specify.

- `boolean`: For this type, the idea is to get the user to answer *yes* or *no*. You can also specify whether there should be a default value:

```
    {
        "type": "boolean",
        "title": "Display Name",
        "description": "Description text",
        "default": false
    }
```

- enum: This one should be thought of as a list of options, which can be useful if you want the user to choose between trips on different dates, for example:

```
    {
        "type": "string",
        "title": "Display Name",
        "description": "Description text",
        "enum": ["option1", "option2", "option3"],
        "enumNames": ["Option 1", "Option 2", "Option 3"]
    }
```

With that in mind, let's see if we can use several of these types, as we will show the implementation parts in the next section.

Implementing the server-side functionality

Let's start with the server. What we need to know is that a server feature, tool, resource, or prompt should run its course, and if it detects that more information is needed, it should produce an elicitation message.

First, let's see how we produce such a message. First, we have an `if` that checks whether a message should be produced. If so, we call `elicit` on the context object while providing a `message` and a schema to abide by:

```
class BookingPreferences(BaseModel):
    """Schema for collecting user preferences."""

    checkAlternative: bool = Field(description="Would you like
        to check another date?")
    alternativeDate: str = Field(
        default="2024-12-26",
        description="Alternative date (YYYY-MM-DD)",
    )


def is_available_date -> bool:
    pass


@mcp.tool()
def book_table(date: str,ctx: Context[ServerSession, None]) -> str:

    # 1. Check if data is available

    if not is_available_date(date):
        result = await ctx.elicit(
            message=(f"No trips available on {date}. Would you
                like to try another date?"),
            schema=BookingPreferences,
        )
```

Then there should be a check to see what the user and the client responded with:

```
if result.action == "accept" and result.data:
    if result.data.checkAlternative:
        return f"[SUCCESS] Booked for {result.data.alternativeDate}"
    return "[CANCELLED] No booking made"
return "[CANCELLED] Booking cancelled"
```

Here, you can see how we investigate the action property to see if the user accepted the primary action and submitted additional data. If so, we start parsing out what was selected. If it wasn't accepted, then we respond with a cancellation message.

Now, let's see it all together:

```python
from pydantic import BaseModel, Field

from mcp.server.fastmcp import Context, FastMCP
from mcp.server.session import ServerSession

mcp = FastMCP(name="Elicitation Example")


class BookingPreferences(BaseModel):
    """Schema for collecting user preferences."""

    checkAlternative: bool = Field(description="Would you like
        to check another date?")
    alternativeDate: str = Field(
        default="2024-12-26",
        description="Alternative date (YYYY-MM-DD)",
    )


@mcp.tool()
async def book_trip(date: str, ctx: Context[ServerSession, None]) -> str:
    """Book a trip with date availability check."""
    # Check if date is available
    if not is_available_date(date):
        # Date unavailable - ask user for alternative
        result = await ctx.elicit(
            message=(f"No trips available on {date}. Would you
```

```
                    like to try another date?"),
            schema=BookingPreferences,
        )

        if result.action == "accept" and result.data:
            if result.data.checkAlternative:
                return f"[SUCCESS] Booked for
                    {result.data.alternativeDate}"
            return "[CANCELLED] No booking made"
        return "[CANCELLED] Booking cancelled"

    # Date available
    return f"[SUCCESS] Booked for {date}"
```

Now, let's move on to testing elicitation features with VS Code.

Testing elicitation with VS Code

To test elicitation features with VS Code, you will need to add the MCP server as an entry to the `mcp.json` file like so:

```
"server": {
    "type": "sse",
    "url": "http://localhost:8000/sse"
}
```

Then, ensure you're in *Agent* mode before you type the following prompt:

```
Book trip on 2025-02-01
```

You should see the following play out in the user interface:

1. **Typing a prompt and tool invocation:** Here, you type your request to book a trip, and the system recognizes it as a tool invocation. You need to approve the tool invocation for it to proceed:

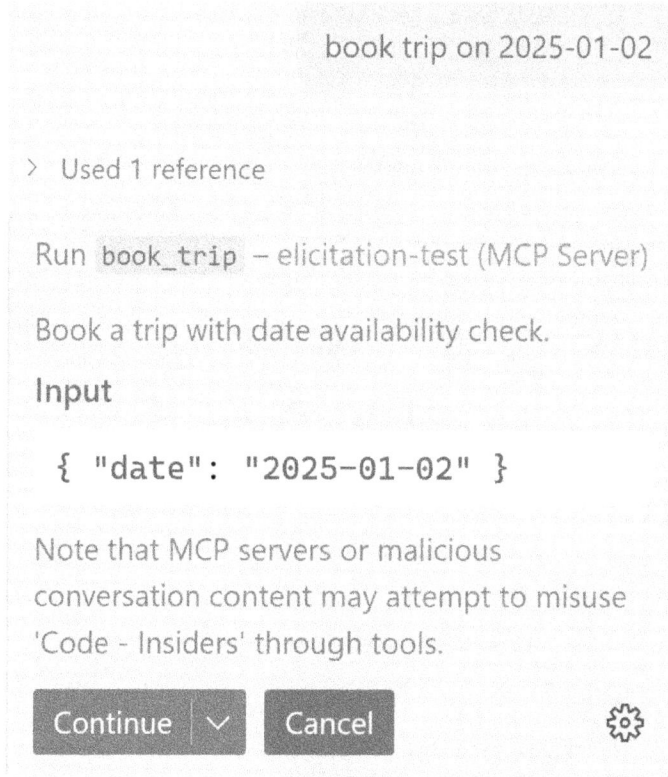

> book trip on 2025-01-02
>
> > Used 1 reference
>
> Run `book_trip` – elicitation-test (MCP Server)
>
> Book a trip with date availability check.
>
> **Input**
>
> `{ "date": "2025-01-02" }`
>
> Note that MCP servers or malicious conversation content may attempt to misuse 'Code - Insiders' through tools.
>
> Continue ⌄   Cancel   ⚙

Figure 10.2 – Typing a prompt and seeing a tool invocation

2. **Approving the tool invocation:** Once you approve the tool invocation, you should see the interface telling you the selected data is busy, and you'll be asked to respond, meaning now it will take you into crafting an elicitation response:

book trip on 2025-01-02

> Used 1 reference

> Running **book_trip** – elicitation-
test (MCP Server)

Request for Input – elicitation-
test (MCP Server)

No trips available on 2025-01-02. Would you
like to try another date?

Respond   Cancel   ⚙

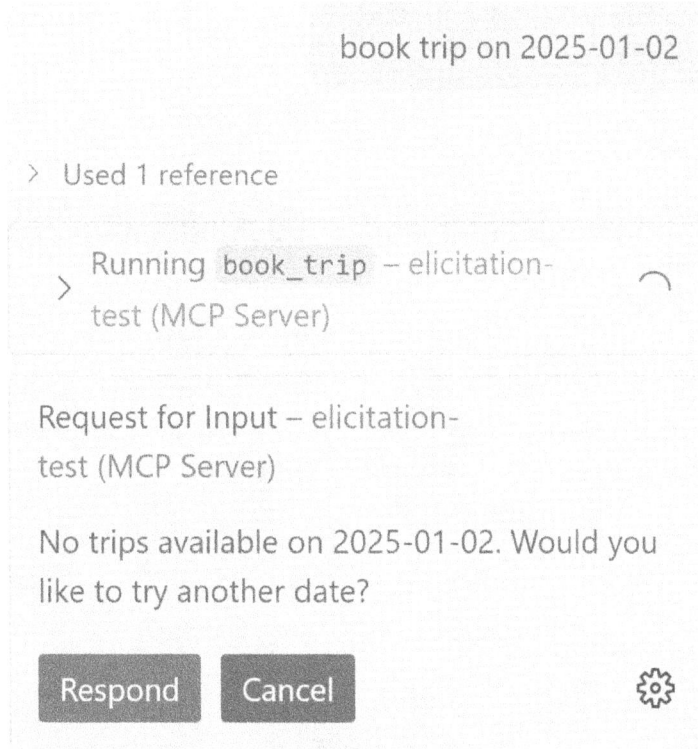

Figure 10.3 – Approving the tool invocation

3. **Crafting an elicitation response**: Now you will need to craft a response based on the user's input and the system's requirements. This involves using the elicitation schema you defined earlier to gather any additional information needed. Here's how that looks in the user interface. In the following screenshot, you're asked whether you want to respond or not. If you choose **true**, it will continue to ask you for another date; if not, it will stop the elicitation process:

Checkalternative (1/2)

Would you like to check another date?

true

false

Figure 10.4 – Crafting an elicitation response

4. **Responding to the elicitation**: Once you've selected to continue, you need to fill in the alternate date like so:

←	Alternativedate (2/2)
2025-01-01	
▶ **2025-01-01**	
None No selection	

Figure 10.5 – Responding to the elicitation

5. **The final result**: Because you've now submitted an alternative date, the server will check to see if this response is okay. In the following screenshot, you can see that that's the case and you receive a confirmation for your booking:

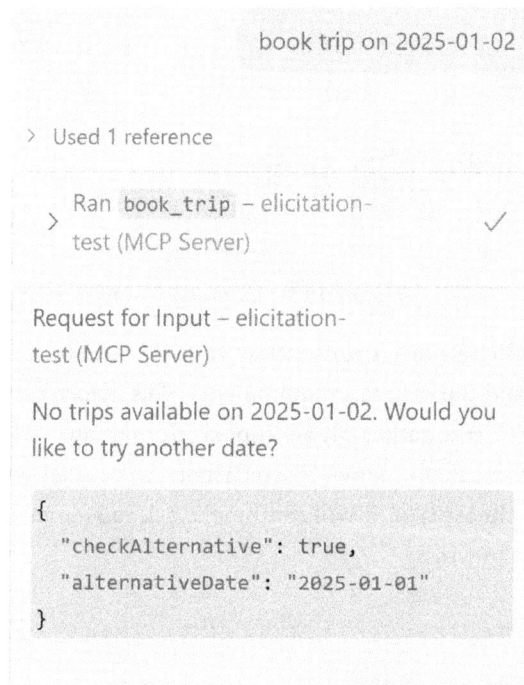

book trip on 2025-01-02

> Used 1 reference

> Ran `book_trip` – elicitation-
test (MCP Server)   ✓

Request for Input – elicitation-
test (MCP Server)

No trips available on 2025-01-02. Would you
like to try another date?

```
{
    "checkAlternative": true,
    "alternativeDate": "2025-01-01"
}
```

The trip has been successfully booked, but it is
scheduled for 2025-01-01 instead of 2025-01-02.
Would you like to change the date to 2025-01-02?

Figure 10.6 – The final result

That completes elicitation on the server side.

Implementing elicitation in the client

Great – now we have a good understanding of the server side of things, and even how to test it with VS Code. Let's proceed to implement the client side.

Normally, when writing a client, you deal with a `ClientSession` object. This allows you to manage the connection to the server. In addition to `read_stream` and `write_stream`, you can also pass `elicitation_callback` to handle any elicitation events:

```
async with ClientSession(
    read_stream,
    write_stream,
    elicitation_callback=elicitation_callback_handler) as session:
```

Let's have a look at `elicitation_callback_handler`:

```
async def elicitation_callback_handler(context:
    RequestContext[ClientSession, None], params: ElicitRequestParams):
    print(f"[CLIENT] Received elicitation data: {params.message}")
```

As you can see, this handler takes two parameters: the request context and the elicitation request parameters. What we need to do at this point is to create a client response that gets sent back to the server. There are three possible responses you can send back to the server:

- `accept`: This means we want the elicitation process to continue. If we give such a response, we should also conform to the input schema set out by the server. For example, the following answer would conform:

  ```
  return ElicitResult(action="accept", content={
      "checkAlternative": True,
      "alternativeDate": "2025-01-01"
  }) # should book 1 jan instead of initial 2nd Jan
  ```

  Here, you see how we first set the `action` property to `accept` and set `content` to a payload, with the schema taking `checkAlternative` and `alternativeDate`. Note also how we hard-code the response. In a more production-like app, the value assigned to `alternativeDate` should come as the result of asking the user for input.

- `decline`: This means we want to stop the elicitation process. We can send a response like this:

  ```
  return ElicitResult(action="decline")
  ```

Here, we don't set content at all, which makes it clear that we are not providing any additional information or context for the decline. This decline response happens very early on in the process. This could be likened to a user simply saying *no* without providing further details.

- accept: The user accepts to respond but then declines to provide an alternative date:

```
# 1. refuses no select other date
return ElicitResult(action="accept", content={
    "checkAlternative": False
}) # should say no booking made, WORKS -->
```

This decline happens a bit later in the process, after the user has been presented with the option to select an alternative date.

Let's try to show it all in this sequence diagram:

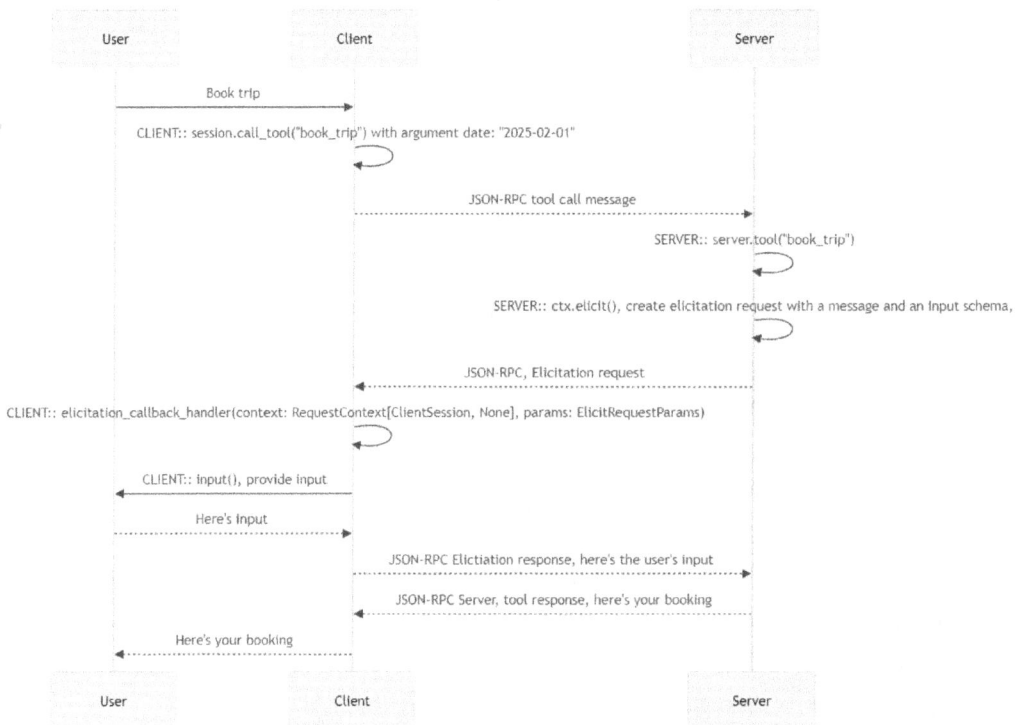

Figure 10.7 – Flow for implementing elicitation in the client in Python

🔍 **Quick tip**: Need to see a high-resolution version of this image? Open this book in the next-gen Packt Reader or view it in the PDF/ePub copy.

📖 **The next-gen Packt Reader** and a **free PDF/ePub copy** of this book are included with your purchase. Scan the QR code OR visit `https://packtpub.com/unlock`, then use the search bar to find this book by name. Double-check the edition shown to make sure you get the right one.

As you can see, generally, there are a few permutations to keep track of where the user can cancel at different stages, but the key is to ensure that the client is able to handle these different scenarios gracefully.

Summary

In this chapter, we've covered the elicitation process in detail, including how it is initiated and the different scenarios in which it can occur. We've also explored the various responses that can be sent back to the server during this process. Elicitation is when the system actively seeks to gather more information from the user in order to fulfill a request or clarify intent.

We've also seen how the user can accept as well as abort at different stages of the process.

Finally, elicitation can be a powerful tool for improving user interactions and ensuring that the system is able to meet user needs effectively.

In the next chapter, we'll explore how to secure your MCP server and client using various authentication methods such as Basic Auth, JWT, and OAuth2.1.

Assignment

So far, you've seen code that handles a booking scenario. Now your task is to implement a scenario where the user finishes a booking process but is asked whether they want to be a member or not to receive a discount for future bookings. Use the code at `https://github.com/PacktPublishing/Learn-Model-Context-Protocol-with-Python/blob/main/Chapter10/code/README.md`.

Solution

You can access the solution at `https://github.com/PacktPublishing/Learn-Model-Context-Protocol-with-Python/blob/main/Chapter10/solution/README.md`.

Quiz

An elicitation process is technically initiated when:

- A: The server determines that it needs more information from the user to complete a request.
- B: The user provides input that requires further clarification or details.
- C: The system needs to confirm user intent before proceeding.

You can access the solution at `https://github.com/PacktPublishing/Learn-Model-Context-Protocol-with-Python/blob/main/Chapter10/solution/solution-quiz.md`.

Unlock this book's exclusive benefits now   **UNLOCK NOW**

Scan this QR code or go to `https://packtpub.com/unlock`, then search this book by name.

Note: Keep your purchase invoice ready before you start.

11

Securing Your Application

In many cases, a prerequisite for a web application is to secure it before you put it in production. There are definitely cases where you don't need to do that, but in most cases, you want to make sure that your application is secure and that only authorized users can access certain parts of it.

Let's look at some scenarios and what security measures you should consider for each of them:

Scenario	Sensitivity level	Security measures	Rationale
Public data that anyone can access	Minimal risk of exposure	Basic security or none	If you want to prevent bots or similar from using your API excessively, opt for having users sign up for an API key
Some public data and some protected data	Moderate risk of exposure	Basic security with HTTPS and API keys	Protect sensitive data while allowing public access to non-sensitive data
Sensitive personal data (e.g., health records and financial information)	High risk of exposure	Advanced security with HTTPS, OAuth 2.0/2.1, encryption, and RBAC	Comply with regulations such as **General Data Protection Regulation (GDPR)** and **Health Insurance Portability and Accountability Act (HIPAA)**, and ensure data privacy and integrity

Table 11.1 – Security measures scenarios

With that in mind, let's look at some common security measures you can implement in your web application.

In this chapter, you will learn how to do the following:

- Add basic authentication to your application
- Secure your application with a **JSON Web Token (JWT)**
- Use OAuth2 to secure your application for an even better security posture

The chapter covers the following topics:

- Basic authentication
- Hardening security with JWT
- How does JWT work?
- Creating a JWT
- Integrating JWT in our middleware (and MCP server)
- OAuth2

Basic authentication

Basic authentication is the simplest way to secure your application. It involves sending a username and password with each request to the server. This is definitely not the most secure way to do it. If it's not that secure, why would you use it? Well, there are scenarios where it's better to have at least *some* security than no security at all. For example, if you have an API and it's generally open to the public but you want to restrict access to certain endpoints, basic authentication can be a good option.

How does it work under the hood? The client sends an Authorization header with each request. The value of this header is the word Basic followed by a space and a Base64-encoded string of the format username:password. The server then decodes this string and checks whether the username and password are valid. Here's the flow of how it works:

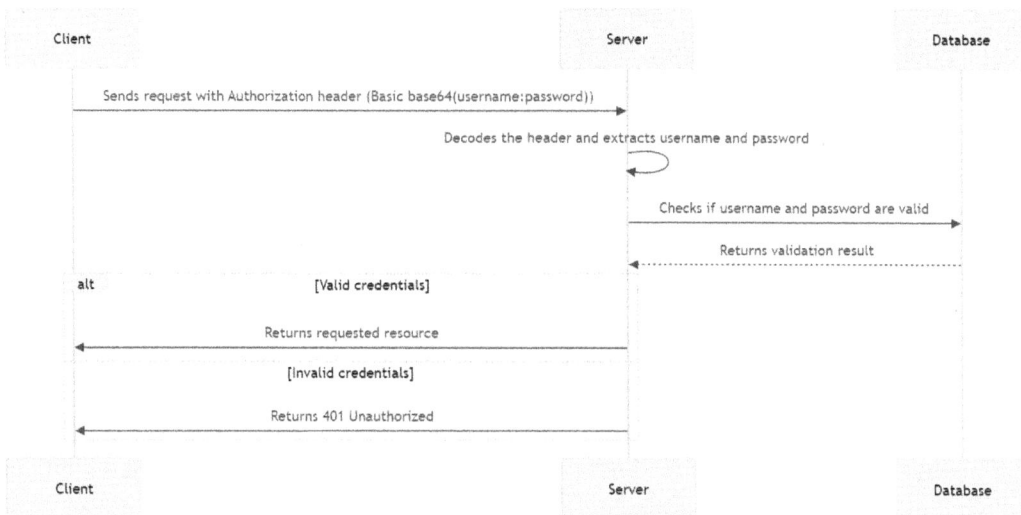

Figure 11.1 – Basic authentication flow

Sometimes the basic authentication consists of an API key instead of a username and password. The API key is sent in the same way as the username and password, but it's just a single string that identifies the client. The server then checks whether the API key is valid.

From a code viewpoint, here's what it can look like when the client sends a request with basic authentication:

```python
# send api key
import requests
import base64

api_key = 'your_api_key'
encoded_api_key = base64.b64encode(api_key.encode()).decode()
headers = {'Authorization': f'Basic {encoded_api_key}'}
response = requests.get('https://api.example.com/endpoint',
    headers=headers)
```

```
print(response.json())
// send api key
const apiKey = 'your_api_key';
const encodedApiKey = btoa(apiKey);
const headers = new Headers();
headers.append('Authorization', `Basic ${encodedApiKey}`);
fetch('https://api.example.com/endpoint', { headers })
    .then(response => response.json())
    .then(data => console.log(data));
```

💡 **Quick tip:** Enhance your coding experience with the **AI Code Explainer** and **Quick Copy** features. Open this book in the next-gen Packt Reader. Click the **Copy** button (**1**) to quickly copy code into your coding environment, or click the **Explain** button (**2**) to get the AI assistant to explain a block of code to you.

```
                                                             Copy      Explain

function calculate(a, b) {
    return {sum: a + b};                                      1           2
};
```

📖 **The next-gen Packt Reader** is included for free with the purchase of this book. Scan the QR code OR go to https://packtpub.com/unlock, then use the search bar to find this book by name. Double-check the edition shown to make sure you get the right one.

Using basic authentication for our MCP server

Let's leverage this technique to secure our MCP server. After all, we don't want just anyone to be able to access our server and potentially misuse it. To get this to work, we need two things:

- A server middleware that checks for the Authorization header and validates the credentials
- The client that sends the Authorization header with each request

Implementing the MCP server and bootstrapping it as a web app

First things first, we need to implement the MCP server and bootstrap it as a web app. In doing so, we will have a web server that can handle MCP requests and responses. Once we're done with this, we can add the middleware to the server that will add the security layer.

This uses Starlette; however, that server isn't easy to get a hold of for your MCP server. So instead, you need to take control of the bootstrapping of the server and add the middleware yourself.

First, let's create our MCP server instance:

```
app = FastMCP(
    name="MCP Resource Server",
    instructions="Resource Server that validates tokens
        via Authorization Server introspection",
    host=settings["host"],
    port=settings["port"],
    debug=True,
)
```

Second, let's see how we can create the Starlette MCP app, which should use the Streamable HTTP transport:

```
starlette_app = app.streamable_http_app()
```

Next, we need the bootstrap code that will run the server. This is done using Uvicorn:

```
async def run(starlette_app):
    import uvicorn
    config = uvicorn.Config(
            starlette_app,
            host=app.settings.host,
```

```
            port=app.settings.port,
            log_level=app.settings.log_level.lower(),
        )
    server = uvicorn.Server(config)
    await server.serve()


run(starlette_app)
```

Creating the middleware

To create our middleware, we need to remember how it should work. The middleware should check for the `Authorization` header, validate the credentials, and either allow the request to proceed or return an error response.

With that in mind, here's what the middleware can look like. We need the middleware itself and a function to validate the token. Middleware in Starlette is created by subclassing `BaseHTTPMiddleware`. It has the request and a `call_next` function that you call to proceed with the request, should the validation be successful. If not, you should return a response with an error code:

```
def valid_token(token: str) -> bool:
    # remove the "Bearer " prefix
    if token.startswith("Bearer "):
        token = token[7:]
        return token == "secret-token"
    return False


class CustomHeaderMiddleware(BaseHTTPMiddleware):
    async def dispatch(self, request, call_next):

        has_header = request.headers.get("Authorization")
        if not has_header:
            print("-> Missing Authorization header!")
            return Response(status_code=401, content="Unauthorized")

        if not valid_token(has_header):
            print("-> Invalid token!")
            return Response(status_code=403, content="Forbidden")
```

```
        print("Valid token, proceeding...")
        print(f"-> Received {request.method} {request.url}")
        response = await call_next(request)
        response.headers['Custom'] = 'Example'
        return response
```

The logic of the middleware is as follows:

- Check whether the Authorization header is present. If not, return a 401 Unauthorized response.
- Validate the token; if the token is invalid, return a 403 Forbidden response.
- If the token is valid, proceed with the request and add a custom header to the response. We proceed with the request by calling call_next(request), which will pass the request to the next middleware or the actual endpoint handler.

The final part is to add the middleware to the Starlette app:

```
middleware = [
    Middleware(CustomHeaderMiddleware, header_value='Customized')
]

async def main():
    print("Running MCP Resource Server...")
    starlette_app = await setup(app)
    print("Adding custom middleware...")
    starlette_app.add_middleware(CustomHeaderMiddleware)
```

In this code, we create a list of middleware and add CustomHeaderMiddleware to it. Then, in the main function, we add the middleware to the Starlette app using starlette_app.add_middleware(CustomHeaderMiddleware).

Testing the middleware

To test the middleware, we can use the same client code as before, but this time, we need to include the Authorization header with a valid token.

Here's how the client code can look:

```
import requests
import base64
```

```python
def get_auth_token():
    api_key = "my_api_key"
    token = base64.b64encode(api_key.encode()).decode()
    return f"Bearer {token}"


headers = {'Authorization': get_auth_token()}
response = requests.get('http://127.0.0.1:8000/protected',
headers=headers)
print(response.status_code)
print(response.text)
```

To test it with an MCP client, it's the same idea, but we need to know how to pass custom headers with the MCP client. Here's how you can do it.

Here, we use `streamablehttp_client` from the MCP SDK to create a client. We pass the `Authorization` header via the `headers` parameter:

```python
token = "secret-token"


async with streamablehttp_client(
        url = f"http://localhost:{port}/mcp",
        headers = {"Authorization": f"Bearer {token}"}
    ) as (
        read_stream,
        write_stream,
        session_callback,
    ):
        async with ClientSession(
            read_stream,
            write_stream
        ) as session:
            await session.initialize()

            # TODO, what you want done in the client,
            e.g list tools, call tools etc.
```

Let's look at JWT next.

Hardening security with JWT

What's the benefit of JWT rather than basic authentication? Well, with JWT, you can have more granular control over what the client can do. You can include claims in the token that specify what the client is allowed to do. For example, you can include a claim that specifies that the client is only allowed to read data, but not write data. This would look like something like this:

```
{
  "sub": "1234567890",
  "name": "User Userson",
  "admin": true,
  "iat": 1516239022,
  "exp": 1516242622,
  "scopes": ["User.Read"]
}
```

This token payload specifies that the client is allowed to read user data. The server can then check the token and see whether the client has the required scope to perform the requested action. There are a lot of other benefits as well, such as the following:

- **Stateless**: The server doesn't need to store any session information. The token contains all the information needed to authenticate the client.

- **Scalability**: Since the server doesn't need to store any session information, it can easily scale horizontally.

- **Security**: The token can be signed and/or encrypted to ensure its integrity and confidentiality.

- **Flexibility**: The token can include any number of custom claims, allowing for a wide range of use cases.

- **Interoperability**: JWT is a widely adopted standard, making it easy to integrate with other systems and services.

Okay, all of that sounds great, but let's take you through what you need to do to *upgrade* your basic authentication to JWT. First off, let's talk about how JWT works.

How does JWT work?

JWT is a compact, URL-safe means of representing claims to be transferred between two parties. The claims in a JWT are encoded as a JSON object. This JSON object has three parts separated by dots (.):

- **Header:** This typically consists of two parts: the type of the token (JWT) and the signing algorithm being used, such as HMAC SHA256 or RSA. A header typically looks like this:

    ```
    {
      "alg": "HS256",
      "typ": "JWT"
    }
    ```

    Here we see that the algorithm used is HMAC SHA256, and the type is JWT. This information is important for the server to know how to verify the token.

- **Payload:** This contains the claims. Claims are statements about an entity (typically, the user) and additional data. There are three types of claims: registered, public, and private claims. A payload typically looks like this:

    ```
    {
      "sub": "1234567890",
      "name": "User Userson",
      "admin": false,
      "iat": 1516239022,
      "exp": 1516242622,
      "scopes": ["User.Write", "User.Write"]
    }
    ```

    This payload represents a user with an ID of 1234567890, the name User Userson, who is not an admin, and the User.Write and User.Read scopes. The iat claim represents the time the token was issued, and the exp claim represents the time the token expires.

- **Signature:** This is used to verify that the sender of the JWT is who it says it is and to ensure that the message wasn't changed along the way.

Creating a JWT

Okay, so we know what parts we have, but how do we create a JWT? Well, it's actually quite simple. You can use a library to create the JWT for you. Here's how you can do it:

```python
# pip install PyJWT
import jwt
import datetime

def create_jwt():
    header = {
        "alg": "HS256",
        "typ": "JWT"
    }

    payload = {
        "sub": "1234567890",              # Subject (user ID)
        "name": "User Userson",            # Custom claim
        "admin": True,                    # Custom claim
        "iat": datetime.datetime.utcnow(),# Issued at
        "exp": datetime.datetime.utcnow() +
            datetime.timedelta(hours=1),  # Expiry
        "scopes": ["Admin.Write", "User.Read"]  # Custom claim for
            scopes/permissions
    }

    secret = "your-256-bit-secret"
    token = jwt.encode(payload, secret, algorithm="HS256", headers=header)
    return token
```

With this code, you can create a JWT with a header, payload, and signature. The jwt.encode function takes care of encoding the header and payload, and signing the token with the secret. The signature is created as part of the jwt.encode function. Now, the token variable is in Base64-encoded format and can be used as a bearer token in the Authorization header. If you remove the Base64 encoding, you would see that the token consists of three parts separated by dots (.), namely, the header, payload, and signature, as mentioned previously. To decode the token, however, you would see the header and payload in JSON format.

Validating the JWT

We also need to know how to validate the JWT. What we do when we validate is ensure that the token is valid, not expired, and that the signature is correct. That's by no means all we can do, but it's a good start. Here's how you can validate a JWT:

```python
import jwt


def validate_jwt(token: str) -> bool:
    secret = "your-256-bit-secret"
    try:
        decoded = jwt.decode(token, secret, algorithms=["HS256"])
        print("Decoded claims:")
        for key, value in decoded.items():
            print(f"  {key}: {value}")
        return True
    except jwt.ExpiredSignatureError:
        print("Token has expired")
        return False
    except jwt.InvalidTokenError:
        print("Invalid token")
        return False
```

This code checks that the token is valid, not expired, and that the signature is correct. If the token is valid, it prints the decoded claims. If the token has expired or is invalid, it prints an error message.

We mentioned earlier that these structural checks are a good start. What other checks should we do? Here are some ideas of things you can check:

- The iss (issuer) claim to ensure the token was issued by a trusted authority, for example, your auth server.
- The aud (audience) claim to ensure the token is intended for your application. Valid values could be your MCP server URL.
- The nbf (not before) claim to ensure the token is not used before a certain time.
- Scopes or roles, to ensure the client has the required permissions to perform the requested action. Examples of scopes could be User.Read, User.Write, Admin.Read, and Admin.Write, and the roles could be User, Admin, and so on. These look similar, but scopes are typically more granular than roles.

Integrating the JWT in our middleware (and MCP server)

So far, you've seen how we perform basic authentication and check whether a credential is valid as part of our middleware. Now, let's see how we can integrate JWT validation. Our plan is as follows:

- Create a JWT for testing. We will do so with a utility script. In a real-world application, you would get the token from an **identity provider** (**IDP**) such as Auth0, Keycloak, or Entra ID.

- Update the middleware to validate the JWT.

- Update the client to send the JWT in the Authorization header.

Creating a JWT for testing

Here's the utility code we will use to create a JWT token for testing, including functions for generating a JWT and validating it:

```python
import jwt
import datetime

def create_jwt():
    header = {
        "alg": "HS256",
        "typ": "JWT"
    }
    payload = {
        "sub": "1234567890",                 # Subject (user ID)
        "name": "User Userson",                # Custom claim
        "admin": True,                     # Custom claim
        "iat": datetime.datetime.utcnow(),# Issued at
        "exp": datetime.datetime.utcnow() +
            datetime.timedelta(hours=1),   # Expiry
        "scopes": ["Admin.Write", "User.Read"]  # Custom claim for
            scopes/permissions
    }
    token = jwt.encode(payload, "your-256-bit-secret",
        algorithm="HS256", headers=header)
    with open(".env", "w") as f:
        f.write(f"JWT_TOKEN={token}\n")
```

```python
def validate_jwt(token: str) -> str | None:
    secret = "your-256-bit-secret"
    try:
        decoded = jwt.decode(token, secret, algorithms=["HS256"])

        return decoded
    except jwt.ExpiredSignatureError:
        print("Token has expired")
        return None
    except jwt.InvalidTokenError:
        print("Invalid token")
        return None


if __name__ == "__main__":
    create_jwt()
```

In this code, we create a JWT with a header, payload, and signature. The create_jwt function generates the token and writes it to a .env file. Note how the validate_jwt function validates the token and returns the decoded claims if the token is valid.

Updating the client to send the JWT

Let's move on to the client. It will need to load the token from the .env file and send it in the Authorization header. Here's how you can do it:

```python
import os
from dotenv import load_dotenv

load_dotenv()

def get_auth_token():
    token = os.getenv("JWT_TOKEN")
    return f"Bearer {token}"

headers = {'Authorization': get_auth_token()}

# omitted, creating and connecting the MCP client
```

Updating the server middleware to validate the JWT

Finally, we need to update the server middleware to validate the JWT. Here's how we can do it:

```python
from your_jwt_utility import validate_jwt  # import the validate_jwt
    function

```python
from starlette.middleware.base import BaseHTTPMiddleware
from starlette.responses import Response

class JWTMiddleware(BaseHTTPMiddleware):
    async def dispatch(self, request, call_next):
        token = request.headers.get("Authorization")
        if not token or not token.startswith("Bearer "):
            return Response("Unauthorized", status_code=401)

        jwt_token = token.split(" ")[1]
        decoded = validate_jwt(jwt_token)
        if not decoded:
            return Response("Unauthorized", status_code=401)

        # TODO, check things like existing user, scopes etc.

        # Optionally attach user info to request.state
        request.state.user = decoded
        response = await call_next(request)
        return response
```

Now, the middleware checks for the Authorization header, validates the JWT, and either allows the request to proceed or returns a 401 Unauthorized response. We're also leaving a TODO task for you to check things such as existing users, scopes, and so on.
```

OAuth2

We've definitely improved our security posture by moving from basic authentication to JWT. However, there's still room for improvement. **OAuth2** is a widely adopted authorization framework that provides a more robust and flexible way to secure your application.

It allows you to delegate access to your resources without sharing credentials. What that means concretely is that there are three parties involved when accessing a resource:

- **Resource server**: This is the server that hosts the protected resources, in our case, the MCP server
- **Client**: This is the application that wants to access the protected resources, in our case, the MCP client
- **Authorization server**: This is the server that issues access tokens to the client after successfully authenticating the resource owner and obtaining authorization

What about the delegation part? Well, the resource owner (typically the user) can delegate access to the client by granting it an access token. The client can then use this access token to access the protected resources on behalf of the resource owner. This way, the client doesn't need to know the resource owner's credentials, and the resource owner can revoke access at any time by invalidating the access token. This is clearly a better approach than basic authentication. JWT, however, is often used to represent the access token in OAuth2. So the real improvement with OAuth2 is that it represents a complete framework for managing access tokens, including how they are issued, validated, and revoked.

OAuth2.1 code flow

OAuth2.1 is what's supported by the MCP SDK. Or rather, the way it's supported is by providing a middleware that lets you point out the following:

- **The authorization server**: This is used to issue and validate tokens
- **The resource server**: This is where your data lives and is typically your MCP server
- **The scopes you want to request**: This is where you define what access you want to the resource server

Here's what the flow looks like:

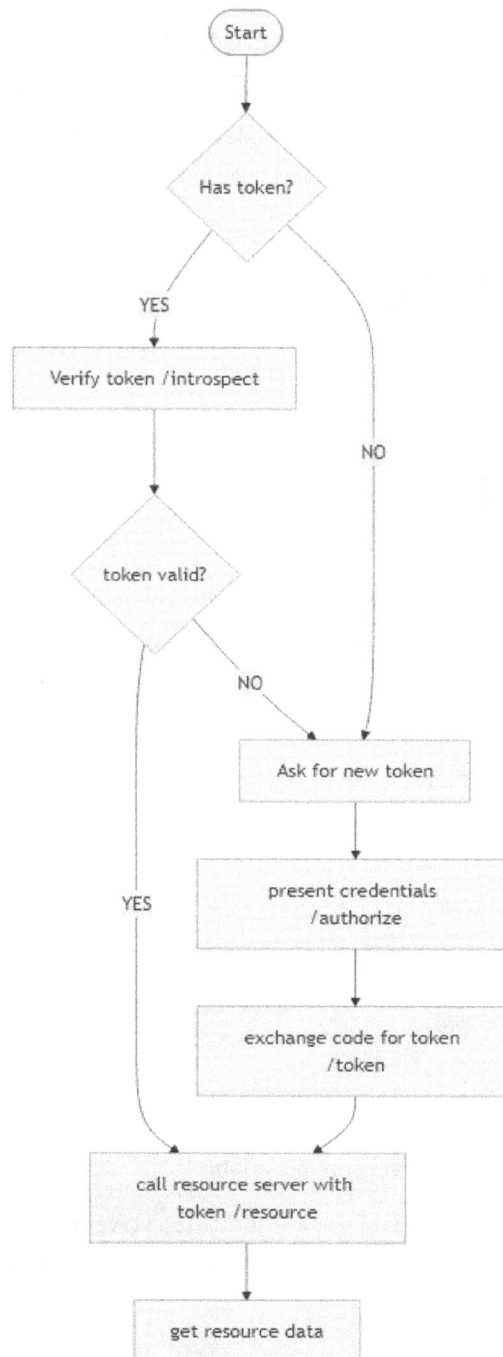

Figure 11.2 – OAuth2.1 flow

🔍**Quick tip**: Need to see a high-resolution version of this image? Open this book in the next-gen Packt Reader or view it in the PDF/ePub copy.

📖**The next-gen Packt Reader** and a **free PDF/ePub copy** of this book are included with your purchase. Scan the QR code OR visit `https://packtpub.com/unlock`, then use the search bar to find this book by name. Double-check the edition shown to make sure you get the right one.

The preceding flow tells us that the client will first check whether it has a valid token. If it does, it will use it to access the resource server. If not, it will ask the user to authenticate and authorize the client to access the resource server on its behalf. Once the client has a valid token, it can use it to access the resource server.

So, what does the MCP SDK do for us then? It provides middleware that lets us easily integrate OAuth2.1 into our MCP server. All we need to do is provide the following configuration options:

```
auth=AuthSettings(
    issuer_url=AnyHttpUrl("https://auth.example.com"),  #
        Authorization Server URL
    resource_server_url=AnyHttpUrl("http://localhost:3001"),  # This
        server's URL
    required_scopes=["user"],
)
```

These are the fields of the middleware configuration:

- `issuer_url`: This is the URL of the authorization server that issues the tokens. In a real-world application, this would be the URL of your IdP, such as Auth0, Keycloak, Entra ID, and so on.

- `resource_server_url`: This is the URL of the resource server, in our case, the MCP server. This is used to validate that the token is intended for this resource server.

- `required_scopes`: This is a list of scopes that the client must have to access the resource server.

This middleware takes care of validating the token, checking the scopes, and ensuring that the token is intended for the resource server. It also handles the OAuth2 flow, including redirecting the user to the authorization server to obtain an access token if needed.

OAuth 2.1 under the hood

To understand how the OAuth2.1 middleware works under the hood, let's explain the OAuth2.1 code flow in more detail. Here's how the flow works:

1. **Validate token or obtain authorization code**: The client checks whether it has a valid access token. If it does, it uses it to access the resource server. If not, it calls the `/authorize` endpoint on the authorization server to obtain an authorization code. This code is obtained when the client presents valid credentials and performs a login. The user is then redirected back to the client with the authorization code.

2. **Call `/token` to exchange authorization code for access token**: The client then calls the `/token` endpoint on the authorization server to exchange the authorization code for an access token. At this point, it's ready to access the resource server.

3. **Access resource server**: Accessing the resource server is done by calling the desired endpoint and providing the access token in the `Authorization` header as a bearer token. The resource server then validates the token, checks the scopes, and ensures that the token is intended for this resource server. If everything checks out, it allows the request to proceed.

Just to get a sense of roughly what code is involved, here's a simplified version of the OAuth2.1 middleware flow:

```
# Step 1: Simulate browser redirect to /authorize
authorize_url = f"{AUTH_SERVER}/authorize?client_id={CLIENT_ID}
    &redirect_uri={REDIRECT_URI}&state={STATE}
        &code_challenge={CODE_CHALLENGE}&code_challenge_method=plain"
print(f"Requesting authorization: {authorize_url}")
response = requests.get(authorize_url, allow_redirects=False)
```

```
# Step 2: Extract authorization code from redirect
redirect_location = response.headers.get("Location")
if not redirect_location:
    print("Authorization server did not redirect. Is it running?")
    exit(1)

parsed_url = urlparse(redirect_location)
query_params = parse_qs(parsed_url.query)
auth_code = query_params.get("code", [None])[0]
print(f"Received authorization code: {auth_code}")

# Step 3: Exchange code for access token
token_response = requests.post(f"{AUTH_SERVER}/token", data={
    "grant_type": "authorization_code",
    "code": auth_code,
    "redirect_uri": REDIRECT_URI,
    "client_id": CLIENT_ID,
    "code_verifier": CODE_VERIFIER
})
token_data = token_response.json()
access_token = token_data.get("access_token")
print(f"Access token: {access_token}")

# Step 4: Call resource server
resource_response = requests.get(f"{RESOURCE_SERVER}/userinfo", headers={
    "Authorization": f"Bearer {access_token}"
})
print("User info response:")
print(resource_response.json())
```

Here's the code explained:

- **Step 1:** The client constructs the authorization URL and makes a GET request to the /authorize endpoint on the authorization server. The user is redirected to this URL to authenticate and authorize the client. The response contains a redirect URL with an authorization code.

- **Step 2:** The client extracts the authorization code from the redirect URL.

- **Step 3**: The client makes a POST request to the /token endpoint on the authorization server to exchange the authorization code for an access token.

- **Step 4**: The client makes a GET request to the resource server, providing the access token in the Authorization header as a bearer token. The resource server validates the token and returns the requested resource if the token is valid.

The MCP SDK provides a sample implementation of OAuth2.1 (https://github.com/ modelcontextprotocol/python-sdk/blob/main/examples/servers/simple-auth/mcp_simple_ auth/auth_server.py) that you're encouraged to check out.

Concluding thoughts on security with OAuth2.1

In a production scenario, the only code you would write yourself would be the client and the resource server. The authorization server would be a separate component/service, for example, handled via Entra ID if you're using Azure, or Amazon Cognito if you're on AWS. Auth0 is another good choice.

You need to decide what you are putting the authorization component in front of:

- **The web server**: If so, you can use standard web server middleware approaches with your chosen IdP, such as Entra ID, Amazon Cognito, Auth0, or similar.

- **The MCP server**: If choosing this, by all means, leverage auth components in the MCP SDK. You can still use standard middleware approaches here as well, but you will use the MCP SDK's built-in authentication features.

- **A gateway (a reverse proxy)**: A gateway is a service such as Azure API Management or Gateway from AWS. Both of these services are capable of handling authentication and can simplify the architecture. Additionally, these services have features you might want to use around AI usage, such as content safety and semantic caching, and also features that help with resiliency and scaling.

Also, when it comes to authorization per tool, you might need to add extra code checks for the call to a tool to ensure that the user has the right scopes/permissions to use that tool. Different tools might require different scopes/permissions. This is not something that's supported out of the box in the MCP SDK, but it's something you can easily add yourself. Something such as the following, where has_permission is a function you implement to check whether the user has the required permission to call the tool:

```
PermissionToolMapping = {
    "User.Read": ["GetUser", "ListUsers"],
```

```
    "User.Write": ["CreateUser", "UpdateUser", "DeleteUser"],
    "Admin.Read": ["GetAdmin", "ListAdmins"]
}

def has_permission(token: str, tool: str) -> bool:
    decoded = validate_jwt(token)
    if not decoded or "scopes" not in decoded:
        return False

    user_scopes = decoded["scopes"]
    required_scopes = [scope for scope, tools in
        PermissionToolMapping.items() if tool in tools]

    return any(scope in user_scopes for scope in required_scopes)

@server.call_tool)
def call_tool((name: str, arguments: dict[str, Any], request:
    types.CallToolRequest) -> types.CallToolResponse:
    if(has_permission(token=request.headers["token"], tool=name):
        # proceed with calling tool
    else:
        raise Exception)
```

Summary

In this chapter, you've learned about the importance of securing your MCP server and client. You've seen how to implement basic authentication, JWT, and OAuth2.1 to enhance the security of your applications. Remember that security is an ongoing process, and it's essential to stay updated with the latest best practices and technologies to protect your applications and data. In our next and final chapter, we'll explore how to bring your MCP server to production and ensure that it's robust and scalable.

Assignment 1: Secure your MCP server with basic authentication

In this assignment, you're asked to implement basic authentication in your MCP server, which involves the creation of a middleware that checks for the `Authorization` header in incoming requests. The client should send the credentials in the `Authorization` header. This is a good first step to secure your MCP server, but remember that basic authentication has its limitations and should ideally be replaced with more secure methods.

Review the code snippets provided earlier in the section on basic authentication for guidance.

Solution 1

You can access the solution at `https://github.com/PacktPublishing/Learn-Model-Context-Protocol-with-Python/blob/main/Chapter11/code/basic/README.md`.

Assignment 2: Secure your MCP server with JWT

In this assignment, you're asked to improve upon your previous assignment by implementing JWT authentication in your MCP server. Review the parts on JWT in this chapter for guidance.

Solution 2

You can access the solution at `https://github.com/PacktPublishing/Learn-Model-Context-Protocol-with-Python/blob/main/Chapter11/solutions/README.md`.

Quiz

What is the most secure approach out of the following?

- A: Basic authentication over HTTP
- B: JWT over HTTP
- C: OAuth 2.1

Which of the following best describes a *scope* in the context of authentication and authorization?

- A: The specific permissions or access rights that a client application is requesting from a resource server.

- B: A unique identifier for a user session

- C: A type of encryption algorithm used to secure tokens

You can access the solution at `https://github.com/PacktPublishing/Learn-Model-Context-Protocol-with-Python/blob/main/Chapter11/solutions/solution-quiz.md`.

Resources

- The whole chapter in this free curriculum tells you about problems, attacks, and how to mitigate them: `https://github.com/microsoft/mcp-for-beginners/tree/main/02-Security`

- This lesson covers Entra ID security with MCP: `https://github.com/microsoft/mcp-for-beginners/tree/main/05-AdvancedTopics/mcp-security-entra`

- This repository shows solutions for working with Azure API Management and OAuth with GitHub: `https://github.com/Azure-Samples/mcp-auth-servers/blob/main/README.md`

- This chapter covers security best practices: `https://github.com/microsoft/mcp-for-beginners/blob/main/05-AdvancedTopics/mcp-security/README.md`

Unlock this book's exclusive benefits now

UNLOCK NOW

Scan this QR code or go to `https://packtpub.com/unlock`, then search this book by name.

Note: Keep your purchase invoice ready before you start.

12

Bringing MCP Apps to Production

Welcome to the final chapter of this book. Great that you've made it this far! You've learned how to build both servers and clients and might be wondering how you take that last step toward sharing what you've built with the world.

That's a great question, and this chapter will guide you through all the things you should consider to ensure that your MCP application is well-tested, reliable, secure, and performs well in a production environment. Let's begin!

This chapter covers the following topics:

- **Architecture and design**: Here, we will go through modular design, integration patterns, and specific architectural impact due to AI

- **Packaging and distribution**: Here, we will discuss different packaging options, standalone, embedded, deployment channels, and semantic versioning

- **Testing and deployment automation**: Here, we will look at different types of testing strategies, such as unit testing, integration testing, and AI testing, and ensure that those tests are used within a CI/CD pipeline to deploy with confidence

- **Operations and observability**: Here, we will talk about scaling, resiliency patterns, observability, governance, and future proofing

Architecture and design

When designing your MCP application, there are several architectural considerations to keep in mind. These include modular design, integration patterns, and the impact of AI on architecture. In this section, we'll look at the following topics:

- **Integration patterns**: How does MCP fit into your existing architecture, and what patterns can you use to ensure seamless integration?

- **Documentation**: How do you document your architecture and design decisions to ensure clarity and maintainability?

- **Architecture review**: What are the key aspects to consider when reviewing your architecture to ensure that it meets your requirements and is scalable, maintainable, and secure?

Now that we have an overview, let's dive into each topic.

Integration patterns

MCP comes with its own set of integration patterns to facilitate seamless communication between clients and servers. However, if you use a transport such as Streamable HTTP or SSE, this server is then hosted via a web app using HTTP and most likely organized like a RESTful API. That could mean you need to develop or use specific middleware for web API-to-MCP communication for the sake of logging, security, and more. Here's how that could work. Note the middleware used in the web API. Also note how the web API is most likely a RESTful API, and the client and server use JSON-RPC, as dictated by the MCP protocol:

Figure 12.1 – Integration patterns flow

In this sequence diagram, you can see how the different components interact with each other. The user makes a request to the web API, which then checks the request against its authentication middleware. If the request is allowed, the web API forwards the request data to the client. The client then communicates with the server using JSON-RPC messages.

Documentation

It's important that we document our code well so we understand all the bigger parts and how they fit together. This will help both current and future developers to understand the system and make it easier to maintain and extend.

Documentation is very important, both for developers and users. Well-documented code is easier to understand, maintain, and use. There are different aspects to consider when it comes to documentation:

- **Document code and generate documentation**: All code should generally be well documented, which means we should aim to document all the operations on input and output. As developers, we know that out-of-date information is sometimes worse than no documentation, so we should strive to generate documentation from the code. What you're looking for is to have your code generate documentation in an Open API format, formerly known as Swagger. For example, this piece of code has its routes documented in a way to make it easy for the used framework to generate documentation from it:

```python
from fastapi import FastAPI
from pydantic import BaseModel
from typing import List

app = FastAPI()


class Booking(BaseModel):
    id: int
    title: str
    description: str = False
    when: str

@app.get("/booking/", response_model=Booking, tags=["bookings"],
    summary="Book a trip",  description="Lets user book a trip[]")
def book_trip():
```

```
return Booking(id=1, title="Trip to Paris", description="A
    wonderful trip to Paris", when="2023-09-15")
```

When the code is documented like so with `tags`, `summary`, and more, this will be used to generate Open API documentation automatically. Whatever framework and runtime you go with, make sure your code is easy to document and easy to generate documentation from.

- **Tests are also documentation**: Tests are sometimes the best way to understand how a feature is supposed to work. They provide concrete examples of expected behavior and can help clarify the intent behind complex logic. Ensure that you include comprehensive tests that cover various scenarios and edge cases.

- **Include context flow diagrams and edge case handling**: Mermaid diagrams are becoming a standard and are also supported by GitHub in terms of rendering various flowcharts, sequence diagrams, and more, so consider Mermaid or another way of creating these diagrams. Seeing how something works visually can save both developers and consumers of the code countless hours.

Architecture review

Your architecture should consider the following:

- **Modular design**: Make sure all functionality is separated into logical boundaries so that all areas are in their own modules. Different runtimes do this in different ways, but a good rule of thumb is that your code should be organized in a way that makes it easy to understand and maintain. Additionally, you should aim to keep related code together and minimize dependencies between modules. Finally, there should only be one reason to change, meaning each module should have a single responsibility. For example, you wouldn't keep parsing logic in the same module as business logic.

- **Validation**: Implement robust validation mechanisms to ensure data integrity and correctness. This includes input validation, output validation, and contract validation between different components. There's also a security aspect to this, as malicious actors may try to exploit vulnerabilities in your system. Python uses Pydantic for data validation and settings management with its MCP SDK Leverage these validation libraries for both input and output to address both correctness and security. Here's an example of using input validation:

```python
from mcp.server.fastmcp import FastMCP
from uuid import uuid4

mcp = FastMCP(name="Tool Example")

from pydantic import BaseModel

class User(BaseModel):
    id: int
    name: str
    email: str

users = []

@mcp.tool()
def create_user(user: User):

    # Create user logic here
    user.id = len(users) + 1
    users.append(user)
    return user

if __name__ == "__main__":
    print("Starting MCP server...")
    mcp.run()
```

In this example, you see that there's a tool called `create_user`. It takes a `User` model as input, which will immediately help with validation and serialization. The following payload would lead to a new user being created:

```json
{
  "id": 0,
  "name": "chris",
  "email": "chris@example.com"
}
```

On the other hand, the following payload would lead to a validation error as id is missing:

```
{
    "name": "chris",
    "email": "chris@example.com"
}
```

This way, you can set up validation for all incoming data and ensure that only correct data enters your system. Of course, from a business and security standpoint, you can keep adding more validation rules as needed before you end up persisting the data.

- **AI's impact on architecture**: If you ship a client and a server, your client will most likely have access to an AI model, which means there are specific things to consider from an architectural standpoint. This includes how the client communicates with the AI model, how to manage context between the client and server, and how to handle any potential failures or timeouts:

  - **Decoupled architecture**: Ensure you decouple content management, model invocation, and the UI.

  - **Latency and reliability, and impact on UI**: Also consider the implications of latency and reliability when designing interactions with the AI model. This means, for example, if the AI model takes time to return a response, ensure that the UI remains responsive and provides feedback to the user. If the AI stops responding due to failure or rate limiting, it needs to be handled gracefully. Also, ensure you have fallback mechanisms such as retry logic and circuit breakers. We'll talk more about this later in the chapter.

  - **Token budgeting**: Not only is the token budget something to consider as a running cost for the AI model, but it's also important from an architectural standpoint, as we will need to implement caching strategies and other mechanisms to optimize token usage.

- **Security**: Implement security best practices to protect your application and its data. This includes securing APIs, managing user authentication and authorization, and ensuring data privacy and compliance with regulations. Consider how you can adopt *least privilege* to minimize access rights for users and services. That means ensuring that users and services only have access to the resources they absolutely need. A consequence of this is that you may need to implement more granular access controls and continuously monitor for any unauthorized access attempts.

Packaging and distribution

Before you even type a single line of code, you need to consider what you're building. With MCP, you have different options on how to package and distribute your application.

Packaging options

Let's look at some packaging options.

- **Standalone server**: This is designed for public access or for private use. Regardless of private or public access, you need to think about authentication, authorization, and data privacy. But for private distribution within a company or organization, you need to think about discoverability, how internal teams will find and use the service, and also compliance with internal policies.

- **Embedded client/server**: Such a system probably consists of a client and a server component, and the client most likely ships with AI capabilities, so make sure you consider the implications of that, such as data privacy and security and responsible AI use, and any regulatory requirements that may apply.

Standalone server

Let's say your goal is to build an MCP server only; that means you most likely focus on building an API that wasn't there before you wrap a pre-existing API. With this being MCP, you need to decide where this server is meant to run. Here are some considerations:

- **Local machine**: In this case, the server needs to use the STDIO transport. Also, because it runs on a user's machine, from a security aspect, how can you ensure it's sandboxed and doesn't have access to resources it shouldn't? In fact, should you even allow it to access the network? That's up to you, but you should consider these aspects. See this filesystem MCP server, where the server comes with configuration that both restricts access, which directories it has access to, and it also ships instructions on how to run it in a container environment to ensure the MCP server has as little access as possible (`https://github.com/modelcontextprotocol/servers/tree/main/src/filesystem`).

- **Remotely via a URL**: If your server is accessed remotely, you might not need to be as much concerned about sandboxing, but you do need to think about authentication and authorization, and every aspect of securing the API endpoint. For authentication/authorization, consider using OAuth2 or API keys, and always validate incoming requests. Additionally, consider **role-based access control (RBAC)** to ensure that users don't have more access to various server features than they need. That is, consider whether you need administrator users, normal users, or guest access, and what resources and what type of permission levels everything should have.

In both of these cases, you're most likely storing the source code in something like GitHub or a similar version-controlled system.

Embedded client/server

Integrating MCP into your existing architecture requires careful planning. From a distribution standpoint, your MCP implementation will most likely deploy in the same motion as your existing services and apps it's integrating with. From a code organizational perspective, you can still create them as separate services callable as APIs or a microservices architecture; the choice is yours. What you do need to realize, though, is that shipping an MCP integration means you ship more than a server; you need to ship an MCP client as well. The client will be responsible for communicating with the MCP server, handling requests, and managing context.

Distribution channels

When it comes to distribution channels, you have a few options:

- **Package the server as a Docker container**: This is a great option if you want to ensure that the server runs in a consistent environment, regardless of where it's deployed. You can push the Docker image to a container registry such as Docker Hub or GitHub Container Registry, and users can pull and run the container easily. With this option, you should specify how to configure the container and any environment variables that need to be set, as in this example:

```
FROM node:22.12-alpine AS builder

WORKDIR /app
```

```
COPY src/filesystem /app
COPY tsconfig.json /tsconfig.json

RUN --mount=type=cache,target=/root/.npm npm install

RUN --mount=type=cache,target=/root/.npm-production npm ci --ignore-
scripts --omit-dev


FROM node:22-alpine AS release

WORKDIR /app

COPY --from=builder /app/dist /app/dist
COPY --from=builder /app/package.json /app/package.json
COPY --from=builder /app/package-lock.json /app/package-lock.json

ENV NODE_ENV=production

RUN npm ci --ignore-scripts --omit-dev

ENTRYPOINT ["node", "/app/dist/index.js"]
```

The preceding example is from the example filesystem MCP server (https://github.com/modelcontextprotocol/servers/tree/main/src/filesystem).

- **Distribute via a package manager**: If your server is built with Node.js or Python, you can package it as an npm module or a PyPI package, respectively. This allows users to easily install and manage your server as a dependency in their own projects. The corresponding package manager for .NET would be NuGet, and for Java, it would be Maven or Gradle. Different package managers have different rules for what's needed to package and distribute your code, but it usually involves the creation of a README file, a license, and compressing the code into a bundle. It's a great way for users of your MCP server to find and use what you've built.

- **Repository distribution**: You can also distribute your server by providing access to the source code repository directly. This allows users to clone the repository and build the server themselves, giving them more control over the build process and dependencies. Make sure you provide instructions on how to run it and configure it. This configuration instruction from Playwright's MCP server (https://github.com/RBC/microsoft-playwright-mcp) is a good example showing how to start using it from a host such as VS Code or Claude Code:

```
{
    "mcpServers": {
      "playwright": {
        "command": "npx",
        "args": [
          "@playwright/mcp@latest"
        ]
      }
    }
}
```

In this instruction, you see how to start the server using npx and how to provide arguments via args.

Adopting semantic versioning

Semantic versioning is another thing we should adopt for our code. This is because it makes it easier for both you and the consumer of your code to understand the nature of changes in each release.

It works with the following versions:

- A major version when you make incompatible API changes
- A minor version when you add functionality in a backward-compatible manner
- A patch version when you make backward-compatible bug fixes

How you encode this in your software is to version your software; for example, in version 1.3.0, 1 is the major version, 3 is the minor version, and 0 is the patch version. If you only fix the software by applying a patch, then you should increment it from 1.3.0 to 1.3.1. Adding a new feature should be seen as a minor, so you would increment it from 1.3.0 to 1.4.0. A lot of changes, including changes that make the code break, are seen as a major change, and the version should therefore increase from 1.3.0 to 2.0.0.

By encoding it this way, you create a clear and predictable versioning scheme that communicates the nature of changes to users and developers alike. Developer teams can therefore choose whether to stay on 1.3.x (in which case, they only update the software due to bug fixes and patch changes), or if they want new features but to prioritize stability, they would instead be okay with any version matching 1.x.x, which would allow them to receive new features while still being on a stable base that doesn't risk breaking changes.

Testing and deployment automation

Testing is a crucial part of software development, and it's especially important when working with AI models. Automated tests help ensure that your code behaves as expected and can catch issues early in the development process. Additionally, deploying your application should be automated to ensure consistency and reliability.

Testing strategy

We've mentioned testing already as a form of documentation. It's also a vital part to ensure the code behaves as expected. Make sure that the tests you write are comprehensive and cover various scenarios. Some tests you might consider include the following:

- **Unit tests:** These are good for ensuring that individual components work as intended. In the context of MCP, consider breaking out parsing logic into separate modules to facilitate easier testing.

- **Integration tests:** These validate the interaction between different components and ensure that they work together as expected. For MCP, if your MCP integration is part of a web application, it could be a good idea to set up end-to-end tests that simulate user interactions with the UI. Such a test would then call a web endpoint, which calls a client, and said client would then call an MCP server feature that processes the request and returns a response.

- **AI tests:** As AI models can behave unpredictably, it's crucial to have tests that specifically validate their outputs. This includes testing for various input scenarios and edge cases, and ensuring that the model's responses are within acceptable parameters. Consider using techniques such as adversarial testing to probe the model's weaknesses. Adversarial testing involves creating inputs that are specifically designed to trick the model into making mistakes. It's also a good idea to have a set of prompts to test against, where the system should work well or should invoke a tool or some other functionality.

Generally, with tests, focus on various aspects such as performance, security, and usability.

Deployment automation

Building an app, securing it, architecting well, and logging... all that is good, but without a robust process for deployment, none of that matters. So what's **robust** then? Robust in the year 2025 means that we can deploy something at the click of a button, many times a day, and that we do so with a number of guardrails in place. **Guardrails** are steps where we ensure that tests run and pass, policies are followed, and we're keeping within certain metrics, for example, we don't make the code slower, and so on.

There are many choices for how to deploy, such as GitHub Actions or Jenkins. They have one thing in common, though: to deploy, you need to define a pipeline with steps in it and make sure the final step leads to an artifact that either can be deployed or you end up with a new deployment in production.

In addition to being able to deploy, we need to ensure that the deployment process is reliable and can be repeated consistently. Also, mistakes happen, so we need to be able to roll back changes if something goes wrong.

What does all this mean for our code? Well, it usually results in a .yml file being created to represent the pipeline mentioned previously.

Then, you might need a different configuration or a different environment, so that's also something to keep in mind.

Is this different for MCP compared to normal software? Well, the difference lies in realizing that you may ship AI, and for that reason, you might need a separate deployment pipeline for your AI, looking at performance on models, context management, and more.

Operations and observability

Once your application is in production, there's a set of problems we need to address:

- **Observability**: Do you know how your app is doing? Is it under load, is it slow, is it failing, and is it secure?

- **Scalability and resilience**: Can your app handle traffic spikes? Can it scale up and down, and is it resilient to failures?

- **Monitoring and feedback**: Do you know when something goes wrong? Can you alert the right people, and do you have a feedback loop to improve the app over time?

- **Governance and compliance**: Are you compliant with regulations? Do you have the right policies in place, and are you managing data responsibly?

- **Future proofing**: Are you prepared for future changes? Can you adapt to new technologies, and are you continuously improving your app?

Observability

Do you know how your app is doing, really? If you do, that means you've been diligent in terms of adding logging, tracing, and metrics. You have probably added a dashboard so you can easily visualize all that, and you even know where to optimize if needed. Most of us aspire to have that level of knowledge of our app and how it's doing. When you develop a piece of software at a business, for a client, and so on, there's a lot at stake. We need to keep the data secure, the app needs to respond at a decent speed and use the resources it's been constrained with, and it needs to work. It doesn't sound that hard, right? But it is, especially when you start serving tens of thousands of customers, or even millions. But instead of focusing on how difficult it is to get all this correct, let's talk about the most important things we need to get in place to at least be able to observe our app:

- **Logging**: Logging is crucial for understanding the behavior of your application. It helps understand what goes in, what went out, and hopefully, how long it took through various parts of the app. Having logging at the right places can help you identify bottlenecks and optimize performance. What's important to consider is the log level (e.g., info, debug, or error) and the context you include (e.g., user ID, request ID, etc.) to make your logs more useful.

- **Tracing**: Tracing is essential for understanding the flow of requests through your system. It allows you to see how different services interact and where bottlenecks may occur. Implement distributed tracing to get a complete picture of request paths and latencies. Tracing differs from logging in that it captures the journey of a request. Therefore, it usually contains additional information such as origin, destination, and any intermediate services involved.

- **Metrics**: Metrics are about knowing the health, performance, and scalability of your server. Important metrics to capture are therefore CPU and memory usage, request throughput, response time, and even error rate. Capturing all that will provide you with a good understanding of how your system is doing.

For observability, MCP isn't vastly different from traditional applications, but there are unique aspects to consider, such as model performance and token usage. What could be of particular interest to measure for MCP specifically could be token usage per request versus when it's being cached or reused. Also, for the sake of logging, MCP has different logs built in that we should leverage to indicate errors, warnings, normal logs, and so on (`https://modelcontextprotocol.io/specification/2025-03-26/server/utilities/logging`).

Scalability and resilience

Another very important aspect of deploying MCP applications is ensuring that they can scale and remain resilient under load. The problem you're solving is to ensure the following:

- **Traffic spikes**: You can take on a sudden increase in traffic without degrading performance. This is usually business-critical if you're an e-commerce company and need to be able to handle an increase in purchases during peak shopping times.

- **Scaling up and down**: You can efficiently manage resources to handle varying loads.

- **Resilience**: You can quickly recover from failures and minimize downtime. Doing this well means the users will barely notice failures or at all. The opposite means the users will experience disruptions and degraded service, and might take their business elsewhere.

Now that we understand the major problems and why we should care about these problems, what's the solution? For traffic spikes, we need to be able to scale up and down quickly. Most cloud providers have this feature built in. What you need to decide on is how much you want to control this. For example, do you want to specify that scaling should happen on a certain CPU or memory load, or are you okay with the chosen platform to handle this?

Also, as an architect, you could also design so that you, for example, use a message queue over directly talking to a database and so on. There are several ways to go about this, and only you know what size you need to account for:

- **Load balancing**: The idea with load balancing is to distribute incoming traffic across multiple instances of your application or service to ensure no single instance is overwhelmed. This improves responsiveness and availability. For the sake of your solution, though, you might treat your application and your AI as separate entities and therefore set up different sets of load-balancing schemes for your MCP server and your AI model endpoints.

- **Rate limiting**: Rate limiting is a technique used to control the amount of incoming requests to a service within a specific time frame. This helps prevent abuse, ensures fair usage, and manages API costs. Again, just like load balancing, you might have different schemes for your web app and your AI endpoints.

- **Circuit breakers**: The idea behind circuit breakers is to detect failures and prevent the system from making requests that are likely to fail. When a certain threshold of failures is reached, the circuit breaker trips, and subsequent requests are automatically rejected for a period of time. This allows the system to recover and prevents it from being overwhelmed by failed requests. From a user experience standpoint, circuit breakers can help maintain a smooth experience by providing fallback options or graceful degradation when certain services are unavailable.

So, how do we implement these mechanisms? Well, some of them can be done at the application level, while others may require infrastructure support. Here are some strategies:

- **Load balancing**: Use a load balancer to distribute traffic across multiple instances of your application or service. This can be done using cloud provider features or dedicated load balancing solutions.
- **Rate limiting**: Implement rate limiting at the API gateway or application level to control the number of requests from users or services. This can help prevent abuse and ensure fair usage.
- **Circuit breakers**: These can be implemented using an API gateway.

If you're using a cloud provider, you should be looking into Azure API Management or Amazon API Gateway to implement these strategies effectively. These services will address security, scalability, and reliability concerns, and even have features helping you with AI concerns. What they have in common is that they use a declarative approach to define these strategies. For example, Azure API Management uses XML to define policies for rate limiting, caching, and other features. That makes it easy to apply and configure without changing any code.

So, the recommendation here is to look into your cloud provider of choice and leverage their API management solutions to implement these strategies. Check the links at the end of this chapter in the *Resources* section for more information.

Monitoring and feedback

For monitoring, we've alluded to the problems you can run into, such as performance bottlenecks, error rates, and user behavior patterns. Here are some strategies to address these issues:

- **Implement application performance monitoring (APM) tools**: Use APM tools to gain insights into performance bottlenecks and error rates.
- **Address error rates**: Implement automated error tracking and alerting to quickly identify and resolve issues.

- **User behavior analytics**: Leverage analytics tools to understand user interactions and identify potential areas for improvement.

- **AI usage**: You want to make sure your AI is used as intended and not being abused or misused, and that it produces the responses you expect. For a solution, you should sample requests and analyze them at regular intervals to ensure compliance with usage policies and performance expectations. Also, add feedback loops in the form of letting users provide input on AI-generated content. Having this in place allows you to perform prompt tuning and context refining. Things you want to set up a system for are also to mitigate prompt injection attacks, unsafe content generation, and other potential risks, such as the mentioning of competitor names and more. Whichever service you end up with should be able to tackle all these.

The major cloud providers have monitoring solutions that can help you set up dashboards, alarms, and more. Also, for AI service usage, there are specialized tools that help you analyze prompts. See more on this in the *Resources* section in this chapter.

Governance and compliance

Governance is about ensuring that your application operates within the bounds of legal and ethical standards. How much you need to adhere to these depends on the sector you work in. There's GDPR for data protection, HIPAA for health information, and other regulations that may apply. Ensure you have a robust compliance framework in place.

From a software standpoint, make it easy to comply with these policies by ensuring you log all interactions and create an *audit trail* so you know who changed what and when. You might also consider implementing access controls and data encryption to further protect sensitive information. If you are shipping AI, you will need to care about bias and fairness in your models. Therefore, you might need things such as robust system prompts and usage of content safety services that help implement the policy you need to adhere to, whether it's GDPR or other regulations.

Future-proofing

Okay, so you've managed to deploy a system that meets your current needs. But what about the future? How can you stay safe, secure, compliant, and whatever else you define as success?

MCP is a fairly young protocol, and as such, it will continue to evolve. You need to keep track of such changes; if there are no constructs you should apply, perhaps there are transports you should stop using (SSE is already deprecated in favor of Streamable HTTP). There might also be new guidance on certain feature usage. You need to stay on top of all of that.

There's also tooling associated with MCP (for example, the Inspector tool) that may change, with either more tools or how you interact with it changing.

Then, you have the SDKs, as software, which are continuously changing. Some changes are so major that they might break your code. You might consider staying on a certain major version at least for a while, but ensure you get all security updates. Combine this with recognized tools such as Dependabot, GitHub Advanced Security, and more to ensure you make informed choices and know what risks you are taking by staying on a certain SDK version or moving on to a new one.

It's hard to foresee the future, but you can have a responsible stance on heightened security. Software changes quickly, and new threats are detected regularly. Stay informed about the latest security practices and be ready to adapt your system as needed.

Summary

This has been a long chapter with much ground to cover, but hopefully you've felt helped by the guidance provided. As long as you're aware of the problems you face and actively work to address them, then the choice is yours for whether you choose to address them through a library, a cloud service, or something else. You should probably spend more time than you think on security, as it's becoming a top concern of companies worldwide.

Make sure you plan according to what you need to do before production, in production, and post-production, and prepare for the future. Stay informed. Things will break; the question is how you respond to those breaks and what measures you have in place to mitigate any potential issues.

If you read this far, it means you've learned a lot from this book, from building your first server and client, interacting with an LLM, consuming the server with a tool such as VS Code, and finally, deploying it in a responsible manner. Congratulations! I'm also always happy to connect with you on LinkedIn at `https://uk.linkedin.com/in/christoffer-noring-3257061`.

Resources

Here are some useful resources:

- *API gateway in Azure AI Management*: `https://docs.azure.cn/en-us/api-management/api-management-gateways-overview`
- This is a great repo showcasing how to add many of the features from rate limiting, monitoring, security, and more – *AI Gateway*: `https://github.com/Azure-Samples/AI-Gateway`

Unlock this book's exclusive benefits now

Scan this QR code or go to `https://packtpub.com/unlock`, then search this book by name.

Note: Keep your purchase invoice ready before you start.

13

Unlock Your Book's Exclusive Benefits

Your copy of this book comes with the following exclusive benefits:

⌕ Next-gen Packt Reader

✦ AI assistant (beta)

▣ DRM-free PDF/ePub downloads

Use the following guide to unlock them if you haven't already. The process takes just a few minutes and needs to be done only once.

How to unlock these benefits in three easy steps

Step 1

Have your purchase invoice for this book ready, as you'll need it in *Step 3*. If you received a physical invoice, scan it on your phone and have it ready as either a PDF, JPG, or PNG.

For more help on finding your invoice, visit https://www.packtpub.com/unlock-benefits/help.

> **Note:** Did you buy this book directly from Packt? You don't need an invoice. After completing Step 2, you can jump straight to your exclusive content.

Step 2

Scan this QR code or go to `https://packtpub.com/unlock`.

On the page that opens (which will look similar to *Figure 13.1* if you're on desktop), search for this book by name. Make sure you select the correct edition.

Figure 13.1: Packt unlock landing page on desktop

Step 3

Once you've selected your book, sign in to your Packt account or create a new one for free. Once you're logged in, upload your invoice. It can be in PDF, PNG, or JPG format and must be no larger than 10 MB. Follow the rest of the instructions on the screen to complete the process.

Need help?

If you get stuck and need help, visit `https://www.packtpub.com/unlock-benefits/help` for a detailed FAQ on how to find your invoices and more. The following QR code will take you to the help page directly:

Note: If you are still facing issues, reach out to `customercare@packt.com`.

Appendix: Building for the Web with Modern Python

This is for those of you who want to learn about using Python and its modern constructs. You might have just switched to Python due to everyone using it because of AI, or maybe you're fairly new to programming. Regardless, a hearty welcome; this appendix is for you. The goal with it is to make sure that when you read the other chapters, you understand all the constructs used and can use them to your benefit.

Type hints and data modeling

Even though Python doesn't enforce types, it definitely benefits from them. Type hints can make your code more readable and help catch errors early.

Here's some code without a type hint on adding a product to a basket:

```python
basket = []

def add_product_to_basket(product):
    basket.append(product)
```

While this code works, it lacks clarity on what type of product is being added to the basket. There's also a risk that we make a mistake when accessing product attributes. You should therefore consider using type hints.

Improved code with type hints

Type hints greatly help your IDE tooling, making it easier to catch errors and understand code. They also help with readability. Type hints such as str, int, and so on just work without the need to add a library. There's also the typing library, which brings in additional types such as List and Optional, for example.

The code shown previously can be made a lot more readable using type hints:

```
from typing import List, Optional


basket: List[dict] = []


def add_product_to_basket(product: dict) -> None:
    basket.append(product)
```

This is a lot better as product is now clearly a dictionary and basket is a list of dictionaries. We can improve this even more by making product into a class, like so:

```
from typing import List


class Product:
    def __init__(self, id: int, name: str, price: float):
        self.id = id
        self.name = name
        self.price = price


basket: List[Product] = []


def add_product_to_basket(product: Product) -> None:
    basket.append(product)
```

What's even better than this? The answer is a library such as **Pydantic**.

Adding Pydantic

So, what problems do we have that warrant using a validation library? Here are a few:

- **Ensuring data integrity** to ensure that the data being processed is accurate and reliable
- **Reducing boilerplate code**, as it can automatically generate validation logic

- **Providing clear error messages**, making it easier to debug issues
- **Simplifying complex data validation logic**, allowing for more maintainable code

Without Pydantic

Imagine for a second that you have data coming in from a web request; the data is in the form of a dictionary, but needs to be a specific type, so we need to convert it to fix it. Here's our situation in Python code:

```python
product_dictionary = {
    "id": 1,
    "name": "Sample Product",
    "price": 19.99
}


class Product:
    def __init__(self, id: int, name: str, price: float):
        self.id = id
        self.name = name
        self.price = price


def from_dict(data: dict) -> Product:
    return Product(
        id=data["id"],
        name=data["name"],
        price=data["price"]
    )


def service(data: dict) -> Product:
    product = from_dict(data)
    # Here you would typically save the product to a database
    return product


p = service(product_dictionary)
print(p)
```

Here, we have a situation where the data is in a dictionary shape, `product_dictionary`, but we need to convert it to a specific type, `Product`. We need to create a `from_dict` function to handle this conversion. This is where Pydantic shines, as it can help us validate and parse this data easily.

With Pydantic

Enter Pydantic, and let's see how we can leverage it for our use case. By inheriting from `BaseModel`, we can create a model that automatically validates and parses our input data. See the following example where we define a `Product` model:

```python
from pydantic import BaseModel


class Product(BaseModel):
    id: int
    name: str
    price: float


product_dictionary = {
    "id": 1,
    "name": "Sample Product",
    "price": 19.99
}


product = Product(**product_dictionary)
print(product)
```

With the preceding code, we have eliminated the need for a manual conversion function. Pydantic takes care of validating and parsing the input data, ensuring that it conforms to the expected structure. This not only simplifies our code but also makes it more robust and easier to maintain.

But there's a problem here: if we feed the dictionary with incorrect data types or missing fields, Pydantic will raise a validation error. This code will crash, in fact, so let's see how we can ensure that we capture any validation errors.

Converting with confidence

If the dictionary doesn't conform to the expected structure, Pydantic will raise a validation error, making it clear what went wrong. Let's make sure we capture any validation errors:

```python
from pydantic import ValidationError, BaseModel
```

```
class Product(BaseModel):
    id: int
    name: str
    price: float

product_dictionary = {
    "id": 1,
    "name": "Sample Product",
    "price": 19.99
}

try:
    product = Product(**product_dictionary)
    print(product)
except ValidationError as e:
    print("Validation error:", e)
```

With this code, we wrap our call to Pydantic in a try-except block to handle any validation errors gracefully. Pydantic does more than just take strings, numbers, and Booleans; it can also handle more complex data types such as lists and dictionaries.

More advanced objects

Let's look at a slightly more complex example featuring a professor and their office hours availability:

```
from pydantic import BaseModel, ValidationError
from typing import List, Dict

professor_dictionary = {
    "id": 1,
    "name": "Dr. Smith",
    "office_hours": [
        {"day": "Monday", "from_": 9, "to_": 12},
        {"day": "Wednesday", "from_": 14, "to_": 17}
    ]
}

class OfficeHour(BaseModel):
```

```
        day: str
        from_: int
        to_: int

class Professor(BaseModel):
    id: int
    name: str
    office_hours: List[OfficeHour]

professor = Professor(**professor_dictionary)
print(professor)
```

In this code, we define a `Professor` model that includes an ID, name, and a list of office hours. Each office hour is represented by an `OfficeHour` model, which includes the day of the week and the start and end times. This structure allows us to easily validate and work with complex data types using Pydantic.

Serialization

Sometimes we have a situation where we need to go from a Pydantic model instance back to a dictionary. This can be useful for serialization or when we need to interact with APIs that expect data in a specific format. For this, we can use `model_dump`, a method that exists on each model. Here's how to use it:

```
from pydantic import BaseModel
from typing import List, Dict

class OfficeHour(BaseModel):
    day: str
    from_: int
    to_: int

class Professor(BaseModel):
    id: int
    name: str
    office_hours: List[OfficeHour]

professor_dict = {
    "id": 1,
```

```
    "name": "Dr. Smith",
    "office_hours": [
        {"day": "Monday", "from_": 9, "to_": 12},
        {"day": "Wednesday", "from_": 14, "to_": 17}
    ]
}

professor = Professor(**professor_dict)

professor_serialized = professor.model_dump() # {"id": 1, "name":
    "Dr. Smith", "office_hours": [{"day": "Monday", "from_": 9,
    "to_": 12}, {"day": "Wednesday", "from_": 14, "to_": 17}]}}

print(professor)
print(professor_serialized)
```

You can even decide what fields are being included using model_dump(include=...) and model_dump(exclude=...):

```
print(m.model_dump(include={'foo', 'bar'}))
#> {'foo': 'hello', 'bar': {'whatever': 123}}
print(m.model_dump(exclude={'foo', 'bar'}))
```

Pydantic is used heavily in MCP internally in the SDK, and you're encouraged to use it for input and output validation.

You can even write our own validators, but I'll leave that as an exercise for you. See the official docs at https://docs.pydantic.dev/latest/concepts/validators/.

async and await

Validating code is important, but another important aspect we also need to understand is asynchronous programming. Asynchronous programming allows us to write code that can perform multiple tasks at once without blocking the main thread. This is particularly useful in scenarios where we need to handle I/O-bound operations, such as making API calls or reading from a database.

Let's talk about **async/await**, which is a syntax for writing asynchronous code in Python. You should use async/await when you want to write non-blocking code that can handle many tasks at once. If your code is blocking, then the end user experience suffers, as they have to wait for each task to complete before moving on. Imagine the problem multiplying on a web server with many users. Okay, so what do we need to know? First, let's start with the concepts:

- coroutine: A so-called coroutine is created when you mark up a function with async def. That means this function can be paused and resumed, allowing other tasks to run in the meantime. Let's see this pause and resume behavior in the following code:

```
import asyncio


async def fetch_data():
    await asyncio.sleep(1)
    return {"data": "some data"}
```

In this code, we define fetch_data, a function marked with the async keyword. The function itself calls await asyncio.sleep(1), meaning we want the code to *stop* here for one second. Then, we *resume* and return a dictionary. Is this non-blocking? Yes, because when asyncio.sleep is running, other work can take place.

- **Event loop**: The event loop is what runs the coroutines and manages their execution. To interact with the event loop and run your async code, call asyncio.run(fetch_data()):

```
import asyncio


async def main():
    data = await fetch_data()
    print(data)


asyncio.run(main())
```

Another way to talk to the event loop is by calling asyncio.get_running_loop(). This will give you the current event loop instance:

- await: You've seen this in use already, but any function marked with async should use await when it's called.

- asyncio: We showed this already by calling its run method. It is a library in Python that provides support for asynchronous programming. It allows you to write concurrent code using the async/await syntax. You'll often use asyncio when working with web frameworks such as FastAPI.

  Let's see a web application example using FastAPI:

  ```python
  from fastapi import FastAPI


  app = FastAPI()

  async def fetch_data():
      await asyncio.sleep(1)
      return {"data": "some data"}


  @app.get("/data")
  async def get_data():
      data = await fetch_data()
      return data
  ```

- asyncio.gather: asyncio provides another useful method called gather, which allows you to run multiple coroutines concurrently and wait for all of them to finish. It's often more convenient than wait when you need the results of all tasks. Here's how to use it:

  ```python
  import asyncio

  async def fetch_data(url: str):
      print("Fetching data...")
      await asyncio.sleep(1)
      return {"data": f" Result from {url}: some data"}

  async def main():
      # Gather multiple coroutines correctly by passing them as
      separate arguments
      results = await asyncio.gather(
          fetch_data("google.com"),
          fetch_data("bing.com"),
  ```

```
                        fetch_data("yahoo.com"),
        )

    print(results)

    asyncio.run(main())
```

Here, each call to fetch_data is passed as an argument to gather. While gather might be more convenient, it does not provide as much control over individual tasks as wait does. Speaking of wait, let's see how it works.

- asyncio.wait: asyncio has useful methods, and one such method is wait, which allows you to wait for multiple tasks to complete. This is particularly useful when you want to run several tasks concurrently and wait for all of them to finish. Here's how to use it:

```python
# python
import asyncio
from typing import List, Optional

async def search_task(name: str, delay: int, workload: List[int],
        find_value: int, stop: asyncio.Event) -> Optional[str]:
    try:
        print(f"Task {name} started")
        await asyncio.sleep(delay)              # simulate I/O
        if stop.is_set():
            return None
        for no in workload:
            await asyncio.sleep(0)              # yield to allow
                cancellation
            if no == find_value:
                stop.set()
                return name
        return None
    except asyncio.CancelledError:
        print(f"Task {name} cancelled")
        raise

async def main():
    stop = asyncio.Event()
```

```
    tasks = [
        asyncio.create_task(search_task("A", 3, [1,2,3], 2, stop)),
        asyncio.create_task(search_task("B", 1, [4,5,6], 2, stop)),
        asyncio.create_task(search_task("C", 5, [7,8,9], 2, stop)),
    ]

    try:
        for finished in asyncio.as_completed(tasks):
            res = await finished
            if res:
                print("Found in", res)
                break
    finally:
        for t in tasks:
            if not t.done():
                t.cancel()
            await asyncio.gather(*tasks, return_exceptions=True)

asyncio.run(main())
```

Here, the code creates three search tasks, each with a different delay and workload. The tasks are started concurrently using asyncio.create_task. The asyncio.as_completed function is used to process the results as they finish. If a task finds the target value, it sets the stop event, which cancels the other tasks. Finally, all tasks are awaited to ensure proper cleanup.

As you can see, there's a lot of flexibility in how you can manage concurrent tasks in Python using asyncio. Let's just mention one more thing: so far, you've seen how your methods can be made async, and even your web frameworks. There's also a specific library for making web requests async, called httpx.

httpx is a fully featured HTTP client for Python 3 that provides async capabilities. It allows you to make HTTP requests in an asynchronous manner, making it a great choice for I/O-bound tasks. Here's a simple example of how to use httpx with async:

```
import httpx
import asyncio

# make a web request to google.com
```

```
async def fetch_web_page(url: str) -> httpx.Response:
    async with httpx.AsyncClient() as client:
        return await client.get(url)

async def main():
    response = await fetch_web_page("https://www.google.com")
    print(response.status_code)

asyncio.run(main())
```

Great, now that we have a better grasp on `async`, let's see how we can use it in a web context.

Uvicorn: the ASGI server

First, let's see where we came from, namely, WSGI. **WSGI** stands for **Web Server Gateway Interface**, a standard interface between web servers and Python web applications. It has been the de facto standard for Python web applications for many years. However, the **Asynchronous Server Gateway Interface** (**ASGI**) was introduced to address the needs of modern web applications, particularly those requiring asynchronous capabilities. So, with ASGI, we can handle asynchronous requests more efficiently in a way we couldn't with WSGI.

Uvicorn is a lightning-fast ASGI server implementation, using `uvloop` and `httptools`. It's perfect for serving your FastAPI applications and can handle both HTTP and WebSocket protocols. `uvloop` is a fast implementation of the event loop, which is the core of asynchronous programming in Python. `httptools` is a library for parsing HTTP requests and responses. Uvicorn works seamlessly with FastAPI and can, for example, start a server, enabling your application to handle requests concurrently. Here's a web server example:

```
#main.py

from fastapi import FastAPI

app = FastAPI()

@app.get("/")
async def read_root():
    return {"Hello": "World"}
```

You can run this FastAPI application with Uvicorn using the following command:

```
uvicorn main:app --reload
```

What the preceding code does is to run a file called main.py and look for an instance of the FastAPI application called app. It will then start the server and enable hot-reloading, so any changes you make to your code will be automatically applied without needing to restart the server.

You can also specify additional options such as the host and port:

```
uvicorn main:app --host 0.0.0.0 --port 8000
```

This is just the beginning of using Uvicorn, but it's a good start to be able to create MCP servers using transports such as SSE or Streamable HTTP.

Context managers

Another thing you will see a lot when working with the MCP SDK is the use of context managers, so what are those? A context manager is a Python object that defines the runtime context to be established when executing a with statement. The most common use case is resource management, where you want to ensure that resources are properly acquired and released. For example, it's a good idea to use it if you need to set up a resource such as a database connection or some other type of resource. Here's a simple example:

```
with db_resource("sqlite.db") as conn:
    # Perform database operations
    pass
```

What makes us able to use the with keyword, you might ask. Well, context managers are able to use the with keyword because they implement two special methods: __enter__ and __exit__. When the with statement is executed, the __enter__ method is called, and when the block inside the with statement is exited, the __exit__ method is called. This allows for setup and teardown actions to be performed automatically. Let's see how the preceding class implements these methods:

```
class db_resource:
    def __init__(self, db_name):
        self.db_name = db_name

    def __enter__(self):
        # Code to establish the database connection
        self.conn = sqlite3.connect(self.db_name)
```

```
        return self.conn

    def __exit__(self, exc_type, exc_value, traceback):
        # Code to close the database connection
        if self.conn:
            self.conn.close()
```

The preceding code demonstrates the use of a context manager for managing database connections. You can see how the __enter__ method establishes the connection and returns it, while the __exit__ method ensures that the connection is closed when the block is exited, even if an exception occurs.

There's another version of with, namely, async with, which is used for asynchronous context managers. These are particularly useful when working with asynchronous code, such as when using asyncio or handling asynchronous I/O operations. The SDK uses this pattern in the client, for example, to make the initial server connection, like so:

```
server_params = StdioServerParameters(
    command="python",
    args=["server.py"]
)


async with stdio_client(server_params) as (read, write):
```

In this code, it now calls the __aenter__ and __aexit__ methods of the asynchronous context manager, which helps to create a server connection. If you keep looking at the SDK code for the client, you will see that the full initialization code looks like so:

```
async with stdio_client(server_params) as (read, write):
        async with ClientSession(read, write) as session:
            # do something with session
```

What's going on here? Two asynchronous context managers are being used in tandem. The outer context manager (stdio_client) is responsible for managing the standard input/output streams for the server connection, while the inner context manager (ClientSession) is responsible for managing the lifecycle of the client session itself. From an implementation standpoint, here's some dummy code:

```
class stdio_client:
```

```python
    def __init__(self, params):
        self.params = params

    async def __aenter__(self):
        self.read, self.write = await self._create_client()
        return self.read, self.write

    async def __aexit__(self, exc_type, exc_value, traceback):
        await self._cleanup()

    async def _create_client(self):
        process = await asyncio.create_subprocess_exec(
            self.params.command, *self.params.args,
            env=self.params.env,
            stdin=asyncio.subprocess.PIPE,
            stdout=asyncio.subprocess.PIPE,
            stderr=asyncio.subprocess.PIPE
        )
        return process.stdin, process.stdout

    async def _cleanup(self):
        pass

class ClientSession:
    def __init__(self, read, write):
        self.read = read
        self.write = write

    async def __aenter__(self):
        # Code to initialize the client session
        return self

    async def __aexit__(self, exc_type, exc_value, traceback):
        # Code to clean up the client session
        pass

    async def initialize(self):
```

```
        # Code to initialize the client session
        pass

async with stdio_client(server_params) as (read, write):
    async with ClientSession(read, write) as session:
        # do something with session
        await session.initialize()
```

Note how the __aenter__ method in stdio_client is responsible for creating the client connection and returning the necessary streams, while the __aenter__ method in ClientSession is responsible for initializing the session with those streams. So, now you hopefully understand why the code looks the way it does. That is, some needed initialization is happening when the context manager is created, and some clean up happens when it is exited. If we don't use a pattern like this, it's easy to forget the clean-up part, and we cause a resource leak.

The contextmanager library

The contextmanager library in Python provides a way to create context managers using generator functions. Instead of defining classes with the __enter__ and __exit__ methods, you can use the @contextmanager decorator to turn a generator function into a context manager. Let's see an example of that:

```python
from contextlib import contextmanager
import asyncio

# create a database resource using context manager
@contextmanager
def database_connection():
    conn = create_connection()
    try:
        yield conn
    finally:
        conn.close()

# use it
def main():
    with database_connection() as db:
        # use the database connection
        pass
```

You can see that we don't need to write __enter__ and __exit__, but can instead decorate a function with @contextmanager to achieve the same effect. This library is also used by the MCP SDK to set up context managers for various resources.

uv: your development environment manager

Let's cover our last topic in this appendix, namely, uv. It's not something you must use, but you're highly recommended to do so. Here's why:

- It provides a consistent interface for managing your development environment. It means you can easily switch between different projects and their dependencies without worrying about conflicts.

- It streamlines the process of setting up and managing virtual environments, making it easier to work on multiple projects with different requirements. So, instead of typing python -m venv env and source env/bin/activate, you can simply use uv init to create and activate a virtual environment, which also initiates your project.

- It simplifies the process of installing and managing dependencies, allowing you to easily add, remove, and update packages as needed. You're used to typing pip install <package> to install a package, but with uv, you can use uv add <package> instead.

- Project management with project.toml is made easier, allowing you to define your project's dependencies and settings in a single file instead of scattering them across multiple files.

- You can even use uv to manage your Docker containers and images, making it easier to deploy your applications in a consistent environment.

Here is what you can do:

1. Install it with the following:

    ```
    pip install uv.
    ```

2. Create a uv configuration file in your project root:

    ```
    uv init
    ```

3. Add a dependency using the uv add command:

    ```
    uv add <package>
    ```

4. Run your app with the following:

    ```
    uv run
    ```

We've come to the end of this appendix. Hopefully, you feel more up to speed with modern Python and tools such as uv, asyncio, and Uvicorn.

Unlock this book's exclusive benefits now

UNLOCK NOW

Scan this QR code or go to https://packtpub.com/unlock, then search this book by name.

Note: Keep your purchase invoice ready before you start.

‹packt›

www.packtub.com

Subscribe to our online digital library for full access to over 7,000 books and videos, as well as industry leading tools to help you plan your personal development and advance your career. For more information, please visit our website.

Why subscribe?

- Spend less time learning and more time coding with practical eBooks and Videos from over 4,000 industry professionals
- Improve your learning with Skill Plans built especially for you
- Get a free eBook or video every month
- Fully searchable for easy access to vital information
- Copy and paste, print, and bookmark content

At www.packtpub.com, you can also read a collection of free technical articles, sign up for a range of free newsletters, and receive exclusive discounts and offers on Packt books and eBooks.

Other Books You May Enjoy

If you enjoyed this book, you may be interested in these other books by Packt:

Node.js Design Patterns, Fourth Edition

Luciano Mammino and Mario Casciaro

ISBN: 978-1-80323-894-4

- Understand Node.js basics and its async event-driven architecture
- Write correct async code using callbacks, promises, and async/await
- Harness Node.js streams to create data-driven processing pipelines
- Implement trusted software design patterns for production-grade applications
- Write testable code and automated tests (unit, integration, E2E)
- Use advanced recipes: caching, batching, async init, offload CPU-bound work
- Build and scale microservices and distributed systems powered by Node.js

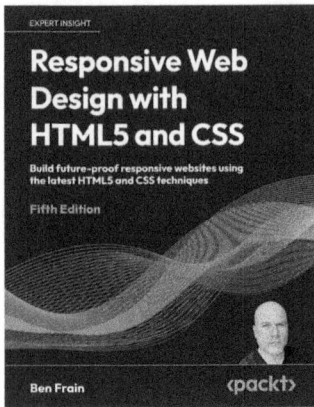

Responsive Web Design with HTML5 and CSS, Fifth Edition

Ben Frain

ISBN: 978-1-83702-823-8

- Leverage color functions to mix colors and convert between color spaces
- Use media and container queries to detect touch/mouse and color preference
- Leverage HTML semantics to author accessible markup
- Use SVGs to provide resolution-independent images and learn to efficiently display them
- Create animations as items enter and leave the viewport using just CSS
- Discover CSS custom properties and make use of new CSS functions
- Add validation and interface elements to HTML forms
- Check whether the frontend code produced by AI tools is effective for your goals

Packt is searching for authors like you

If you're interested in becoming an author for Packt, please visit authors.packtpub.com and apply today. We have worked with thousands of developers and tech professionals, just like you, to help them share their insight with the global tech community. You can make a general application, apply for a specific hot topic that we are recruiting an author for, or submit your own idea.

Share your thoughts

Now you've finished *Learn Model Context Protocol with Python*, we'd love to hear your thoughts! Scan the QR code below to go straight to the Amazon review page for this book and share your feedback or leave a review on the site that you purchased it from.

https://packt.link/r/1806103230

Your review is important to us and the tech community and will help us make sure we're delivering excellent quality content.

Index

www.ingramcontent.com/pod-product-compliance
Lightning Source LLC
Chambersburg PA
CBHW081054220326
41598CB00038B/7092